MODE ONE

Let The Women Know What You're REALLY Thinking

Alan Roger Currie

Mode One Enterprises
Hollywood, CA 90046

MODE ONE

Let The Women Know What You're REALLY Thinking

Alan Roger Currie

ACKNOWLEDGMENTS

This endeavor would have never happened if it were not for the support of my late father, Clarence R. Currie; my mother, Mildred R. Currie; my brother, Stephen C. Currie; my cousin, Jason P. Jones; my close friends Timothy Beverly, DeMarrio Gray, Jeff Kenton, Cory Pulliman, Blake F. Scott, and Maurice L. Taylor.

Others, over the years, who have supported this effort have been: Adrienne Yates, Keith Olivetti, James Parker, Shenille L. Lucy, Kimberly Brown, LaVeta Hughes, Wendy English, Allison Dean, Troy Perry, David Thompson, Dr. Roxanna E. Harlow, Cheryl Ponton, Dr. Francine Fields, Buddy Lewis, Chi Blackburn, Greg Hines, Arnold Reed, Philip Pulliam, Carleton Lewis, Felicia Griffin, Sheri Barker, Ervin V. Pulliam III, John Soo Hoo, Tiffany Kennedy, Rebecca Smith, Kimberly Jones-Snipe, Anthrice Bray, Harold Leonard, Leo Lagrier, Dianthia Simon, Kimberley Ashley, Atha Baugh, Nathan Stewart, Rachelle, Marlon Scott, and Tracie M. Johnson.

There are some authors, and/or other "well-known" celebrity types, who I really don't know personally, but I was influenced and/or inspired by them, and their work: Steven R. Covey, Dr. Brad Blanton, Dr. Susan Campbell, Rom Wills, John Leslie, Anthony Spinelli, Anthony Spinelli Jr., Dr. Harriet Braiker, Susan Forward, Susan Jeffers, Kelly Bryson, the late Richard Pryor, Warren Beatty, Jack Nicholson, Jon Favreau., Alfie Kohn, Michael Baisden, the late James Allen, and Michael Mann.

I know I'm forgetting to mention SOMEONE, SOMEWHERE, who either directly, or indirectly, had some sort of influence on my motivation to write this book. Please forgive me.

CONTENTS

Introduction

First, a word about 'self-improvement' books: Most contain more hype and unsubstantiated 'theories' than they do useful information. At least half of the self-help and self-improvement books I've read left me more confused about what I needed help with, than before I read the book. Realistically though, no one self-improvement book can help you more than **you allow it to help you**. Ideally, what a good self-improvement book seeks to do is provoke you to reexamine those thoughts, attitudes, and beliefs, that you currently hold on to, that are either directly or indirectly, preventing you from achieving your ultimate objectives in life.

I'm different from many authors in the sense that, quite frankly, I did not really want to publish this book. I came up with the Four Modes Of Verbal Communication™ way back in October of 1990, and initially, I just looked at them as my own personal principles for evaluating effective behavior vs. ineffective behavior towards the women I was meeting. I noticed that I never felt angry, frustrated, or bitter towards women, even if they failed to reciprocate my interests, whenever I exhibited what I now refer to as **Mode One Behavior**. On the other hand, just about every time that I exhibited either Mode Two Behavior and/or Mode Three Behavior, I seemed to always feel angry, egotistically frustrated, resentful, and even sometimes, misogynistic towards the entire female gender, in those instances where my relationships or interactions didn't work out the way that I had desired them to.

Then, in 1996 while my brother was working in San Diego, he had two young men who worked for him who were having problems with women. One had moved from Wisconsin, and was pretty much 'striking out' with women on a regular basis,

1

despite being a man of good looks and intelligence. The other had broken up with his ex-girlfriend a few months prior, and had become somewhat reclusive and reluctant as far as meeting and dating new women. My brother told them about my Mode One principles, which at the time was simply in the form of a 25-30 page informal pamphlet. They both expressed a high degree of skepticism. "You can't just tell women what you're REALLY thinking ... what you REALLY want from them ... you just can't do that. At least, not in your very first conversation with them."

In Dr. Brad Blanton's book, *Radical Honesty*, he makes the assertion that we have become a nation full of liars. I can't say that I disagree with this statement. I actually have met many men who believe that the #1 key to having success with women is to LIE to them. Tell them 'what they want to hear,' even if it's dishonest or insincere. They perceive this as "getting over" on women. What a shame.

Of all the various aspects of men's and women's behavior that contribute to poor, short-lived relationships, persistent dishonesty has to be at the top of the list. I think what led me to discover the Four Modes Of Verbal Communication™ is that I noticed whenever I went out of my way to be 'liked' by women, and tell women 'what they wanted to hear,' I never got anywhere. On the other hand, whenever I've been totally and unconventionally *straightforward* with women, I've usually received the responses and reactions that I desired.

Needless to say, those two men who worked for my brother ended up reading my pamphlet, and applied the principles to their next few interactions with single women. Within less than two weeks, one of the two men was meeting and dating numerous single women on a regular basis. The other gentlemen met one particular woman he was really interested in romantically, and they connected immediately.

They both came back to the office telling my brother, "You have to tell Alan to publish this as a book!! This Mode One stuff works!" After receiving a few more words of encouragement from male friends and acquaintances, I finally said "What the heck." And so here it is. The book that is fifteen years overdue.

To eliminate any potential for unsubstantiated 'hype,' I'm going to tell you right now what many books that emphasize improving your success in attracting women won't tell you: **You cannot make a woman who is not interested in you, become interested in you**. The vast majority of these 'how to pick up women' type books, and 'how to get any beautiful woman you want in your bed' type books tend to mislead you into believing that you have the "magic power" to virtually attract any single woman you meet. NOT TRUE. Take me for example. If I'm just flat out, 100% not interested in a woman, there is very little, if anything that this woman can do to 'make me' interested in her. Realistically, it's just not going to happen. That's the 'bad' news.

The **good news** is that there are many women who hide and/or deny the fact that they are really attracted to you, and interested in dating you and/or having sex with you. For every two women who you meet who will straightforwardly acknowledge that they are interested in you, there are probably another 3-5 women who are interested in you, but will temporarily or indefinitely *pretend* as though they're not. These are the women who Mode One Behavior primarily targets.

In my opinion, dating in society would be less challenging, less confusing, and less frustrating if everyone was just REAL with one another. The #1 problem with today's dating climate is that there are too many men and women who are phony, manipulative, and/or very duplicitous in their behavior. Men and women are so obsessed with pleasing everyone, and

3

leaving them with a "good impression," that we have become a society full of "pleasantly phony" people-pleasers. And in the long-run, this creates a high degree of passive-aggressive behavior in people, and in particular, men.

Don't read the whole book in one sitting. Read one chapter at a time, and then stop and reflect on your past interactions and relationships with women. Jot down some notes on a scrap piece of paper. Then continue. After reading this book, your attitude and demeanor will become a lot more calm, cool, and collected. Your manner of verbal expression will become a lot more honest, self-assured, and straightforward. **You will be a different man**. And women will undoubtedly notice this.

Welcome to the world of MODE ONE Behavior.

CHAPTER ONE

Breaking Through The "Small Talk" Barrier: Why We Approach And Interact With Women In The First Place

"Men today are a mere shadow of what they could be. Many men are putting on a façade to get along in life. Many are wearing masks to conform to the social and political climate. This is especially the case when men deal with women."
Rom Wills, author of <u>Nice Guys And Players: Becoming The Man Women Want</u>

Small talk. I absolutely **hate** small talk. Why do we engage in what's known as "small talk" (i.e., conversation that is trivial and meaningless, but usually, to some degree, entertaining) when most of us really don't care for it? Because we're being *pleasantly phony*, with the objective of making those who we're conversing with feel as comfortable around us as possible.

Since I was a child, I was conditioned by my elders, and particularly my female elders, to always be 'well-mannered' and tactful. To be the "little gentleman." I was groomed to always exhibit behavior that was pleasing and flattering to whomever I was speaking with. It was a given that you avoided saying anything that had the potential to be insulting, controversial, or too personal. It has been my experience that most men who were raised in a middle-class, two parent, church-going family were generally groomed in the same manner.

As I grew older, I began to develop a certain degree of ambivalent feelings about my well-mannered behavior. Specifically, in regards to interacting with women. How many times have you observed a guy who was frequently criticized, in one way or another, by a reasonably large percentage of the women who were acquainted with him, but that same guy was never at a lack for romantic and sexual companionship? Or, on the contrary, how many times have you observed a male friend of yours (you maybe?) who was repeatedly complimented on how much of a "gentleman" they were, how much of a "sweetheart" they were, how funny and entertaining they were, and how fun to be around they were . . . BUT . . . this guy was always struggling to maintain the romantic and sexual interest of women? For better or for worse, I have had the interesting perspective of experiencing BOTH sides of that social coin. The former situation was never a problem, but the latter situation was always frustrating to me.

What I began to slowly, but surely come to realize was that, generally, the women who had the highest degree of romantic and sexual interest in me were those women with whom I behaved in a very natural, relaxed, self-assured, and egotistically indifferent manner. In other words, I was **REAL** with them, and I didn't really care whether or not those women 'liked' me, or approved of my behavior. On the flip side though, most of the women who I had very disappointing and frustrating interactions with were generally those who I tried too hard to be "Mr. Perfect Gentleman": Always trying to say the 'right' thing, do the 'right' thing, and generally communicate with them in a manner that was exceptionally pleasing and flattering to that woman's ego.

I truly believe that deep down, all men want to consistently exhibit what I would categorize as **"Mode One Behavior."** The one factor that probably prevents men from doing so is also the one factor that probably has the most detrimental effect on our day-to-day, week-to-week behavior while interacting with others:

THE FEAR OF WHAT OTHER PEOPLE ARE GOING TO THINK AND SAY ABOUT OUR BEHAVIOR.

Think about it. How many times have you been around friends, family, and/or social acquaintances, and have felt the desire to exhibit free-spirited, uninhibited behavior, only to be held back by the paralyzing fear of being criticized, 'looked at funny,' reprimanded, disliked, or causing others to feel uncomfortable?

I've been in this position too many times to mention. I've definitely been guilty of this in the company of **new female acquaintances** more so than in the company of new male acquaintances. I generally always 'speak my mind' around males, regardless of whether I've known them for two years or two hours. Expressing myself in a candid, extremely straightforward manner in the company of desirable women has always been more of a challenge for me, and based on the many conversations I've had with other men, I found that I was definitely not alone.

THE PRIMARY BASIS BEHIND THE FOUR MODES OF VERBAL COMMUNICATION™

Here is the fundamental truth regarding most male-female interactions: **WE ALL WANT SOMETHING.** The biggest lie you can tell yourself when you approach a woman who you're romantically and/or sexually interested in is that you "don't want anything" from this woman. **YES YOU DO.** Just about everybody who we interact with on a regular or semi-regular basis, we have a need and/or desire that we would like to see fulfilled and satisfied. What we desire can be something intangible such as flattering attention or respect. It can be something tangible such as a monetary favor or an offer of employment. Bottom line ... very rarely, if ever, do you approach a woman "just for the heck of it."

Most of my adult life, my behavior had always vacillated between being confident, forthright, and provocative, and being well-mannered, cautious, and indirect. But prior to Fall of 1990, I had never actually thought to "categorize" my behavior, or anyone else's behavior. It wasn't until an interaction I had one evening in October of 1990, with a young lady who was acquainted with my mother, that I first came up with what is now known as **The Four Modes Of Verbal Communication™**.

That evening, I had a chance run in with this woman who was more familiar with my mother than myself. Now, as I alluded to earlier, this was the very type of woman who I usually had the most problems being my "real" self around. Anytime a young lady mentioned that she knew "Mrs. Currie," my brain would immediately provoke me to exhibit behavior that was totally representative of being "Mr. Perfect Gentleman." Sure enough, we ended up initially engaging in about fifteen to twenty minutes of uninteresting, irrelevant "small talk." **And you KNOW how much I HATE SMALL TALK.**

Why do men frequently engage in trivial, meaningless small talk with women with whom they're attracted to, when they know that this type of conversation is usually ineffective and unproductive? Because they are either a) **confused** about what it is they really want from this woman (a relationship? casual sex? a platonic friendship?), or b) they know **specifically** what they want, but they are *afraid* to communicate this to women. In my experiences and observations, it's usually the latter.

This is what basically distinguishes the difference between **effective** verbal communication and **ineffective** verbal communication. When you know what you want from women, and you communicate your needs and desires to them in a confident, honest, and clearly understandable manner, this is representative of *effective verbal communication*. On the other hand, when you're confused about what it is you really want from women, or you know exactly what you want from women, but you are afraid to communicate this information to them, this is representative of *ineffective verbal communication*.

When I was conversing with this young lady who was acquainted with my mother, I knew **exactly** what I wanted from her. I wanted to have casual sex with her. She was physically attractive, and had a very sexy demeanor about her. Was it shallow or superficial on my part to want to have [casual] sexual relations with her so quickly? Maybe, maybe not. Is it to your long-term detriment to interact with women in a phony, ineffective manner, while attempting to "hide" your true desires, interests, and intentions from them? **MOST DEFINITELY**.

Now some people would argue that introducing the idea of having sex with a woman in your *very first conversation* with her is "socially inappropriate," or at minimum, representative of "bad manners." They would contend that this type of conversational behavior is not representative of a true "gentleman." **I DISAGREE.** In my opinion, there is a fine line difference between exhibiting behavior that is *socially appropriate*, and behavior that is *phony* and *insincere.* I think the former has value most of the time, but the latter leads to ineffective and unproductive relationships with women. I'm not at all suggesting that any man should be intentionally 'rude' or 'disrespectful' towards women. That won't get you anywhere. On the other hand though, you want to avoid making comments, and expressing desires and interests that are not representative of what you're **REALLY** thinking.

That's my definition of "real" behavior. **REAL behavior is behavior that is representative of your true and honest needs, thoughts, desires, interests, and intentions.** On the contrary, **PHONY behavior is behavior that gives people a deceitful and/or misleading impression of what your true needs, thoughts, desires, interests, and intentions are.** If I interact with you primarily because I want you to help me find a job, and everything about my behavior allows you to know clearly that this is my main objective, I'm being **real** with you. On the other hand, if I interact with you, and I give you the impression that I just want to "enjoy your company and conversation," when in reality, I want you to introduce me to someone who can help me land a job, I would be guilty of being **phony** and **manipulative**.

Returning to my conversation with the young lady in 1990, my frustration finally reached a breaking point. I couldn't take any more of this unproductive "small talk" any longer. I abruptly interrupted her while she was talking, and finally communicated to her in a very *bold, ultra-confident,* and *extremely straightforward manner* what my <u>real</u> desires, interests, and intentions were (I let her know I wanted to have casual sex with her). **THE MANNER IN WHICH I EXPRESSED MYSELF TOTALLY CAUGHT HER OFF GUARD.**

"Excuse me??! I beg your pardon??!"
As anticipated, my bold, extremely provocative, and straightforward manner of expression threw her for a loop. *"Excuse me?!?!"* was her first response. *"I beg your pardon?!?!"* came next. *"I cannot believe you just said that!!"* immediately followed. Now if I had received those types of shocked and flabbergasted responses from any other woman who was acquainted with my mother prior to this night, I might have been tempted to immediately become apologetic and regretful. **Afraid** that my "Mr. Perfect Gentleman" reputation would possibly be tarnished. But on this night … in this conversation … I

COULD CARE LESS. The desire to be REAL outweighed my desire to maintain an "innocent," "wholesome," and/or "well-mannered" image.

"Do you talk like this to ALL WOMEN in your very FIRST CONVERSATION with them?!?!" was the question she asked. My response? "What difference does it make to you how I approach other women ... the important thing right now is that I approached **you** in the manner that I did because I'm interested in getting together with **you**."

HER SURPRISING RESPONSE

She paused. She then just sat in my car for a moment and stared out the window. I figured after expressing to her why I REALLY wanted to share her company, either one of two things was about to happen: a) she was going to express to me, in one way or another, that she was uncomfortable with my provocative, straight-to-the-point manner of expressing myself, and convey to me that she had no desire in sharing my company in the near future; OR b) she was going to slowly, but surely acknowledge that the idea of us getting together wasn't so bad after all, and subsequently invite me to share her company in the very near future (hey, it had happened before). After a few more moments of silence, she finally chose the latter response.

She gazed at me with a look of amazement and admiration, and soon let me know that she was *incredibly turned on* by my ultra-bold approach, my highly self-assured demeanor, and my fearlessly straightforward manner of verbal communication. Once she relaxed, she confessed that even when she was behaving in a shocked and startled manner, deep down, she actually found my manner of expression *highly appealing.* In particular, she acknowledged that once she realized that I wasn't going to *wimp out* and apologize for expressing my desires and interests in such an unconventionally straightforward manner, she became *even more turned on. "That is how I've always wanted a man ... at least, one who I'm physically attracted to ... to talk to me. But realistically, I would never expect most men to have the guts to ... at least, not in their very first conversation with me..."*

LIGHT BULB ON TOP OF THE HEAD TIME

That comment she made about me saying "what she *wanted to hear,* but *wouldn't* [normally] *expect to hear*" intrigued me. After about 20-30 minutes of kissing and making out in the car, she wrote down her number and told me to feel free to come by her place the next day.

When I got home that evening, I was like a man on a mission. I was so excited that I had conquered my fear of *speaking my mind,* and risking my "Mr. Perfect Gentleman" reputation, that I didn't know what to do. The fact that I had aroused her sexually was irrelevant and secondary. For me, the biggest thing was *avoiding engaging in small talk, and feeling as though I was being phony.* I had an adrenaline rush that was <u>incredible</u>. The biggest thing was that I kept repeating that comment in my head: "what she **wanted to hear,** but **didn't expect to hear.**"

Beginning with that night, and on through the weekend, I began reading magazine articles on male-female relationships, books on what men and women found appealing and arousing in each other, and listening to men and women on TV talk shows talk about good and bad first date experiences. I began to think about all of my own experiences with women, as well as some of the experiences of most of the males who I was close friends with. After days of thought, I finally came to the conclusion that *all conversational behavior* exhibited by men towards women who they're attracted to generally falls into one of four categories:

• Saying what women generally **WANT TO HEAR,** but for the most part, <u>**DON'T**</u> **EXPECT TO HEAR** (primarily, because they don't think you have the "guts" to say what's really on your mind); I categorized this behavior as **"Mode One Behavior."**

• Saying what women generally **WANT TO HEAR,** and also what they generally **EXPECT TO HEAR** (primarily, because you're being "well-mannered" and "conventional"); I categorized this behavior as **"Mode Two Behavior."**

• Saying what women generally **DON'T** WANT TO HEAR, but what they typically **EXPECT TO HEAR** (primarily, because everything you're saying is phony, insincere, timid, and/or cliché); I categorized this behavior as **"Mode Three Behavior."**

• Saying what women generally **DON'T** WANT TO HEAR, and also what they **DON'T EXPECT TO HEAR** (primarily, because you're being rude, crass, insulting, and/or blatantly disrespectful); I categorized this behavior as **"Mode Four Behavior."**

And thus, THE FOUR MODES OF VERBAL COMMUNICATION™ were born.

But why is Mode One Behavior **necessary**? What makes it so **effective**? Read on.

CHAPTER TWO

Manipulative "Game Playing": Why Men Frequently Feel Angry, Frustrated, And Bitter Towards Women

"I will always try to manipulate men and dominate them egotistically ... always. Why? Because it's fun, and because I can. If I'm successful, I will play them for everything they have to offer until I get bored. If I can't, and I'm attracted to them, I will pursue them relentlessly until they're mine."
A female making a confession in the popular women's magazine, ESSENCE

Generally speaking, I typically evaluate all behavior exhibited towards others from two primary perspectives: *Strong Behavior VS Weak Behavior,* and *Effective Behavior VS Ineffective Behavior.* As I emphasized in the previous chapter, we all are interested in having some sort of need and/or desire fulfilled and satisfied when we interact with others, and in particular, women who we have some degree of romantic and/or sexual interest in.

STRONG BEHAVIOR vs WEAK BEHAVIOR

One of the dictionary definitions of the term "strong" is "incapable of being easily damaged, destroyed, or broken down; securely fixed, firm" I define **strong behavior** as behavior that is very firm in its principles and values. When you exhibit strong behavior, it is virtually impossible for you to be easily manipulated or taken advantage of. When you interact with people who have principles and values that are in stark contrast to your own, their behavior will have very little, if any influence on how you behave.

Weak behavior on the other hand, is behavior that is easily affected by the opinions and influence of others. Any time another person can easily provoke you to change, modify, and/or compromise your principles, values, and moral character without valid cause, then this is representative of weak behavior. Similarly, if you're a person who can very easily and frequently be manipulated by others, disrespected by others, or egotistically dominated by others, that means your behavior is weak.

EFFECTIVE BEHAVIOR vs INEFFECTIVE BEHAVIOR

The dictionary definition for "effective" is "capable of producing an intended or desired result." So basically, **effective behavior** is representative of any behavior that you exhibit that has the potential to produce the results that you ultimately desire. If your primary desire is to provoke a woman to share your company in a romantic manner, and the behavior you're currently exhibiting has the potential to lead to that objective, then you're exhibiting effective behavior.

If the behavior which you exhibit is frequently counterproductive to your desired goals and objectives, then this means that your behavior is ineffective.   **Ineffective behavior** is synonymous with unproductive, time-wasting behavior.   Any time you're exhibiting behavior that has very little, if any chance of leading to the results that you desire, you're wasting time in an unproductive manner.

Quick Recap:

Strong Behavior: Any form of behavior you exhibit that makes it virtually impossible for others to manipulate you, disrespect you, and/or cause you to change or compromise your personal principles and values without a valid purpose;

Weak Behavior: Any form of behavior you exhibit that makes it fairly easy for others to manipulate you, disrespect you, and/or provoke you to change or compromise your personal principles and values without valid cause;

Effective Behavior: Any form of behavior you exhibit that is highly conducive to the achievement of your desired goals and objectives;

Ineffective Behavior: Any form of behavior you exhibit that is generally counterproductive to the achievement of your desired goals and objectives.

It's these various forms of behavior that contribute to what distinguishes the four modes of behavior. The "starting point" of all relationships with women begins with one basic concept:

What it is you really want from women, and how do you go about choosing to communicate this to them.

In my experience with women, as well as my observation of other men's experiences, I would tend to distinguish all behavior towards women into four basic categories:

- Behavior that is **strong AND effective;** This is representative of MODE ONE BEHAVIOR.

- Behavior that is **weak, BUT effective;** This is representative of MODE TWO BEHAVIOR.

- Behavior that is **weak AND ineffective;** This is representative of MODE THREE BEHAVIOR.

• Behavior that is **strong, BUT ineffective;** This is representative of MODE FOUR BEHAVIOR.

MODE ONE BEHAVIOR IS ABOUT CONQUERING YOUR FEARS

I have found that the primary factor that distinguishes Mode One Behavior from Mode Two Behavior, Mode Two Behavior from Mode Three Behavior, and so on, basically revolves around the *__degree of fear__ you have towards letting women know **what it is that you really want from them**; Why you **really** want to **share their company.***

When you exhibit Mode Two Behavior, your primary fear is...

• **THE FEAR OF HARSH, SUBJECTIVE CRITICISM**

(i.e., the fear of having a woman express "disapproval" of your real desires, interests, and intentions, OR, the manner in which you chose to verbally communicate them to her)

When you exhibit Mode Three Behavior, your primary fear is...

• **THE FEAR OF BEING REJECTED and/or IGNORED**

(i.e., the fear of not having your real desires, interests, and intentions reciprocated by a woman, and/or the fear of being indefinitely ignored)

When you exhibit Mode Two Behavior, you're not so much concerned with anticipating a negative reaction to **what desires and** *interests you express to women,* but rather **HOW and WHEN you express them.** In other words, when you're in a Mode Two state of mind, you're not afraid to let women know what you want from them, or what you're really thinking, but you tend to be overly concerned with **the manner** in which you verbally express your thoughts and desires to them. This is why I describe Mode Two Behavior as weak, but effective. Mode Two is *effective* primarily because you're being honest with women in regards to what your true needs, desires, interests, and intentions are, but on the negative end, Mode Two Behavior is *weak* because of the manner in which you choose to express your needs and desires is usually too cautious, too delayed, and/or too hesitant and indirect.

When you exhibit Mode Three Behavior, you tend to be more afraid of an adverse reaction to *what desires and interests you're expressing.* When you're in a Mode Three state of mind, you're highly afraid of letting women know what you want from them, or what you're really thinking, because you're afraid that they won't share the same desires and interests that you do. Mode Three Behavior is *weak* because it's predicated on fear. In addition, Mode Three Behavior is *ineffective* because you're hiding, denying, or camouflaging what your true needs, desires, interests, and intentions are.

Many times, you can get away with exhibiting Mode Two Behavior, or even Mode Three Behavior, when you're interacting with people, and women in particular, who are non-manipulative and have your best interests at heart. Realistically though, there are many men and women out in the world who are just looking for the chance to manipulate someone's behavior to serve their own selfish desires. The primary aspect of your behavior that manipulative people prey on, is your **fear** of being either criticized, disliked, rejected, and/or ignored.

It's when a man feels as though he has been taken advantage of, unfairly criticized, and/or blown off or ignored in an unnecessarily harsh manner, that leads him to another mode of behavior known as **Mode Four** Behavior. Mode Four Behavior is not really provoked by any type of fear, but rather it is predicated on a desire for "egotistical revenge" towards a female (either one or two particular females, or the whole gender). **This is over half of the reason why I wrote this book.** To help men eliminate that residual anger, frustration, and bitterness that usually develops after a man feels as though he's been misled, disrespected, or manipulated, by a woman who he was romantically and/or sexually interested in.

Mode Four Behavior is behavior that is **strong, but ineffective.** Mode Four is strong because you're usually being honest and straightforward with women in regard to what your true needs, desires, and interests are, but on the other hand, Mode Four behavior is ineffective because you're only being honest because you're angry, or because you already know that your needs and desires will not be satisfied or reciprocated. When you're in a Mode Four state of mind, you don't really have a genuine interest in sharing a woman's company. You've basically become a misogynist (a man who is physically and sexually attracted to women, but **hates them** as human beings). You will date a woman and/or have sex with a woman primarily for the sake of ultimately hurting them emotionally, or leaving them with a bruised ego.

As I mentioned in the previous chapter, with every woman who you have a desire to approach and interact with, there is **something that you want from them**. Don't fool yourself. I can only laugh when I hear men make statements such as, *"Oh ... I don't really want anything from her..."* **Why are you talking to her then?** *"I just want to share her company and get to know her better..."* **Why?** Most women who you approach, you either want to date them (i.e., spend time with them in a romantic and exclusively committed manner), or you want to have sex with them in a short-term, non-exclusive, casual manner.

If there is one thing that many men don't realize, is that there is a difference between *talking* and *verbally communicating.* Have you heard the adage, "He was talking a lot, but he wasn't saying anything."?? Talking is simply **verbalizing words.** For example, if I read off a list of random words from a sheet of paper, I would be talking, but I wouldn't be *communicating* anything. If you're making comments or statements that don't make any sense, and others have a hard time comprehending what point you're trying to get across, *you're talking, but you're not communicating.*

To verbally communicate means to express and/or exchange **useful information.** If a woman is providing me with information that can help me make choices and decisions regarding my interest in further interacting with her, she is *communicating* with me. Communicating primarily centers around expressing one's physical and emotional **needs,** their **desires,** their general **interests,** and their short-term or long-term **intentions.**

On the next page, I have a matrix of how each **mode of verbal communication** is distinguished. This will give you a better idea of the specific characteristics of each mode of behavior:

ALAN ROGER CURRIE

THE FOUR MODES OF VERBAL COMMUNICATION™

	WHAT WOMEN GENERALLY "WANT" TO HEAR	WHAT WOMEN GENERALLY "DON'T WANT" TO HEAR
WHAT WOMEN GENERALLY "EXPECT" TO HEAR	**MODE TWO** When you express your needs, desires, interests, and intentions to a woman in a cautious, hesitant, indirect, 'beat-around-the-bush' manner Your behavior is usually very polite, considerate, pleasant, entertaining, and non-threatening; You're confident to a degree, but very conscious about your image and reputation among women; You like being known and perceived as a "gentleman" *Big Issue: You have a fear of being harshly criticized and/or disliked; Your main objective is to get a woman to "like" you, and say "nice things" about you, prior to letting her know why you really want to interact with her, and share her company*	**MODE THREE** When you hide, deny, and/or 'camouflage' your true, honest needs, desires, interests, and intentions from women; Your behavior is usually phony, hypocritical, wimpy, deceitful, and 'wishy washy'; You have a low degree of self-confidence and self-esteem, to the point that you will typically allow women to use you, manipulate you, and even disrespect you on a frequent basis *Big Issue: You have a fear of being rejected and/or ignored; You'd rather 'pretend' to be 'just friends' with a female, in order to continue getting attention from her, then to let your real desires and interests be known, and risk being rejected or ignored indefinitely*
WHAT WOMEN GENERALLY "DON'T EXPECT" TO HEAR	**MODE ONE** When you express your needs, desires, interests, and intentions to a woman in a highly confident, unapologetic, straightforward, and very specific manner; Your behavior is usually highly self-assured, composed, non-defensive, and provocative; You don't go out of your way to get women to "like" you, or "approve" of your behavior; You are the personification of "egotistical indifference" *Big Issue: You don't like your time to be wasted by those women who don't have a sincere desire to reciprocate your romantic and/or sexual desires and interests; You don't like to interact with women who are highly manipulative (i.e., "game players")*	**MODE FOUR** When you express your real desires, interests, intentions, and harsh criticisms in a straightforward, unapologetic, and specific manner, but only AFTER you've already been rejected, criticized, or ignored; Your behavior is driven by resentment, misogyny, bitterness, and a desire for "egotistical revenge" towards those women who you feel treated you in a less-than-desirable manner *Big Issue: You don't like to feel 'egotistically defeated' by a woman; When a woman rejects you, criticizes you, or ignores you, you want to gain a measure of emotional and egotistical 'revenge' in the worst way*

26

Most dictionaries define the term "manipulative" as "to directly or indirectly influence another person's behavior in a manner that is usually to one's own advantage (i.e., your interactions with others is more selfishly beneficial rather than mutually beneficial)" That definition is, to a large degree, appropriate and valid, but for this book's purposes, I will slightly modify it. I would generally describe "manipulative" behavior with this definition:

ANY TIME THAT YOU'RE ATTEMPTING TO INFLUENCE and MOTIVATE A SPECIFIC RESPONSE FROM OTHERS THAT IS DESIRABLE and BENEFICIAL TO YOURSELF, THROUGH THE USE OF INCENTIVES and REWARDS, and/or DECEPTIVE, MISLEADING BEHAVIOR, YOU ARE BEING MANIPULATIVE.

In other words, anytime you want something from someone, and you STRAIGHTFORWARDLY ask them for it, that would be representative of *non-manipulative* behavior. But if I want something from you, and I attempt to flatter your ego first, treat you nicely, take you out to dinner, etc., **THEN** ask you for what I want ... that's being MANIPULATIVE. As a man, anytime you begin offering *incentives and rewards* in exchange for romantic and sexual companionship, you are engaging in *manipulative game playing*. Similarly, anytime you lie to women about what you really want from them, and why you really want to share their company, you're engaging in manipulative **head games**.

A long, long time ago, men were guilty of engaging in manipulative game playing when the idea of prostitution was introduced to society. Once men began to offer monetary incentives and rewards to women in exchange for sexual companionship, a whole new element was added to the realm of male-female relationships. Soon, even outside the context of a courtesan transaction, men continued to *compensate* women for sexual favors. Women with manipulative intentions couldn't resist the idea of being offered *incentives and rewards* in exchange for romantic and sexual companionship.

Alfie Kohn, in his book *Punished By Rewards*, clearly points out that once you begin offering incentives and rewards to children, students, employees, women, etc., the interest and excitement towards their respective activity begins to gradually decline. For example, if you consistently offer your children ice cream in exchange for keeping their room clean, after a while, their interest in maintaining a clean room will diminish. Soon, they will be requesting a BMW motor scooter in exchange for keeping their room clean. This holds true to when you consistently offer incentives and rewards to women in exchange for romantic and sexual companionship. Something as simple as **flattery**, is actually an *intangible incentive*. Anytime you offer to "wine & dine" a woman in exchange for her companionship, you're offering an *incentive* as a means of increasing her motivation to spend time with you.

As men, let's be honest. Most men will do JUST ABOUT ANYTHING to attract and maintain the romantic and sexual companionship of an attractive, desirable female. **THAT'S A FACT**. Realistically, nothing will motivate a [heterosexual] man to improve his physical appearance, his level of career success, his education, or his financial status more than the desire to either attract one particular female of interest, or a high number of desirable females. *DON'T THINK FOR A MOMENT THAT WOMEN DON'T KNOW THIS.* This is what gets many of the manipulative games between single men and single women started.

Once a woman knows that you're willing to spoil her and/or attempt to manipulate her (i.e., offer her incentives and rewards in exchange for her companionship), if she's MANIPULATIVE HERSELF, she's going to try to take full advantage of this. *THIS IS WHY <u>MODE ONE</u> <u>BEHAVIOR</u> IS NOT ONLY EFFECTIVE, BUT NEEDED.* If you're offering a woman an expensive dinner and a night at the movie theater as a manipulative tool, eventually, she's going to want to be treated to dinner and a movie **every week**. If you're offering a ride in your Ferrari as a means of enhancing a woman's interest in you, pretty soon, she's going to want **her own Ferrari**. If you're offering a woman the

29

opportunity to have her own condo at your expense, pretty soon she's going to want the house on the beach. TRUST ME MEN: *If you choose to play "The Game," WOMEN WILL PLAY IT BETTER.* Women **KNOW** the game. Men **THINK** they know the game.

Let's say, hypothetically, that all women you interacted with were *non-manipulative*. Meaning, under all circumstances, each and every woman you conversed with either a) straightforwardly communicated to you that they were interested in dating you and/or having [casual] sex with you, OR b) they straightforwardly communicated to you that they had NO interest in dating you and/or having [casual] sex with you.

Dialogue with the opposite gender while in search of a new (or for some, an additional) companion would be a clearly understood, cut and dry, and most importantly, straightforward interaction. Of course, you might experience some occasional rejection and some degree of egotistical disappointment, but **NO HEAD GAMES**.

The problem is, we do not live in an ideal society, and unfortunately, there are women in this society who are **MANIPULATIVE** (not that men aren't; **Men can be VERY MANIPULATIVE as well when they want something from a woman, but are afraid to tell them upfront**).

FEAR always motivates manipulative behavior. When you're afraid to be upfront with your real needs, real desires, real interests, and true long-term intentions and objectives, you're going to be inclined to exhibit manipulative behavior. But what most people don't consciously realize, is that **MANIPULATION IS ALWAYS A TWO-WAY STREET.** "Really??" **YES.**

In other words, **THE ONLY WAY A WOMEN CAN MANIPULATE YOU IS IF YOU'RE EITHER DIRECTLY** (intentionally) **OR INDIRECTLY** (subconsciously) **TRYING TO MANIPULATE THEM.**

When you choose to exhibit **Mode Two Behavior***, or* **Mode Three Behavior***, you're either* consciously *or* subconsciously *attempting to* **MANIPULATE a woman.**

The two primary goals of Mode One Behavior is to . . .

1) *Prevent women from manipulating you and/or disrespecting you;*

2) *Prevent women from wasting your time in an unproductive manner.*

Strong behavior is the key to goal #1, and **effective** behavior is the key to goal #2. What is the key to creating strong, effective behavior towards women? You have to know **WHAT YOU WANT** from women, **WHY YOU WANT IT**, and **WHAT BEHAVIOR you're willing to exhibit** (or **NOT exhibit**) in order to get it.

Earlier in this chapter, I defined strong behavior as behavior that is firm in its principles and values. **THIS IS THE #1 KEY TO IMPROVING YOUR BEHAVIOR TOWARDS WOMEN.** You have to have a definite, specific, detailed list of principles and values that you are not willing to change, sacrifice, or compromise in the process of pursuing the companionship of those women you desire.

For example, let's say that you don't believe in using illegal drugs, such as cocaine. Then, one day you meet this beautiful, sexy woman, and you find out that she is primarily attracted to men who use cocaine, and can provide her with cocaine. So you decide to purchase some cocaine, and invite her to share your company so you two can snort some. *This would be a primary example of you violating one of your own personal principles for the sake of gaining a woman's attention. This is WEAK.*

Dr. Stephen R. Covey, in his popular, best-selling book *The Seven Habits of Highly Effective Behavior*, emphasizes the idea of basing your behavior around your principles and values. He basically says that all of us should have a "personal mission statement" as to what principles and values we're willing to maintain in the process of pursuing and achieving our desired goals and objectives. Once you begin to frequently and consistently violate your own personal principles and values, your character and integrity becomes weak, and you begin to lose credibility and respect in the eyes of others. This is important to remember.

Now I know some men reading this might say to themselves, "what does things like 'character,' 'integrity,' and 'personal values' have to do with attracting women??" **A LOT**. More than the average guy might realize. Believe it or not, it is actually better to consistently maintain principles that are not the most righteous or virtuous, then to frequently "flip flop," and contradict your own principles. For example, if every time you talked to a woman who was against the use of drugs, and you behave as though you support that stance, but then, when you're around women who are attractive and use drugs, you behave as though you condone this, that's **wishy-washy**. Either you're not staying true to your personal principles, or worse, *you don't have any.*

In many surveys conducted, *self-confidence* and *self-assurance* is usually the #1 factor identified that attracts and arouses women, that is not related to physical appearance. **What most men don't realize is that there is a direct correlation between the level of confidence you**

exude towards women, and how true you stay to your personal principles and values.

It is not my place to tell men why they should share women's company. Some men may want a serious, romantic, long-term one-on-one relationship with a woman, while other men may only want a short-lived, casual, purely sexual relationship with a woman. To each his own.

What I try to emphasize and convey in this book is that regardless of what your needs, desires, interests, and intentions are, it's always best to identify them specifically, and communicate them **confidently** and **straightforwardly.** This book will help you do just that.

What is the very first Mode One principle? **NEVER REALLY CONCERN YOURSELF WITH WHAT BOTHERS YOU ABOUT WOMEN'S BEHAVIOR.** Why? Because **you have NO control over changing or improving a woman's behavior. Only she does.**

Only concern yourself with two aspects of <u>YOUR</u> behavior:

1) *"How do I generally behave towards women?"* This is the "proactive" component of your behavior; This is the aspect that centers on how *effective* versus how *ineffective* your behavior is;

2) *"How do I generally allow women to behave towards me?"* This is the "responsive" component of your behavior; This is the aspect that centers on how *strong* versus how *weak* your behavior is.

Don't attempt to manipulate women. Don't allow women to manipulate you. Don't allow women to waste your time if they're really not genuinely interested in you. Don't allow women to engage in "manipulative head games" with you. Be CONFIDENT. Be FEARLESS. Be STRAIGHTFORWARD. Get ready for the freedom of MODE ONE.

Before I explain why Mode One is so strong and effective in preventing manipulative behavior, I will first point out why the other three modes of behavior are so weak and/or ineffective. First though, I want you to perform a brief exercise:

Take out a pencil, and a piece of paper, and think of the last five to ten interactions or relationships you've had with women that resulted in you feeling either a) angry towards that female, b) egotistically frustrated, and/or c) bitter and resentful towards the female gender in general. Then, once you have your list of interactions/relationships, answer these four questions:

1) Did you ever lie to any of these women, or mislead them, in regards to what your true needs, desires, interests, and intentions were?

2) Did you ever hesitate for more than a week before letting any of these women know what your true interests and intentions were?

3) Did you ever suppress satisfying your own emotional needs and egotistical desires for the sake of accommodating any of these women's needs and desires?

4) Were you guilty of expressing your needs, desires, interests and intentions to these women in a manner that was confusing, vague, ambiguous, and/or not totally clear and specific?

Once you answer these four questions, you're free to proceed to Chapter Three.

CHAPTER THREE

The Men who Exhibit Mode TWO Behavior: The "Pleasant Postponers"

"It's not normal to be honest. Normal people are concerned with figuring out the right thing to say that puts them in the best light. They want to live up to their own best guess about what the people they are talking to want to hear." Dr. Brad Blanton, author of <u>Radical Honesty: How To Transform Your Life By Telling The Truth</u>

Mode Two Behavior. This is the behavior that is probably the most frequently exhibited towards women by single men than any of the other three "modes" of behavior. Why? Because most men have been conditioned (see Chapter One) to leave women with a "good impression," and to do and say those things that are most representative of being a gentleman. These men want to maintain a positive, favorable, wholesome reputation with just about every female they come in contact with.

As I mentioned in the previous chapter, all behavior you exhibit towards others, and particularly women, is either strong or weak, and effective or ineffective. Mode Two Behavior is behavior that falls into the category of *weak*, but [usually] *effective*. Most men who exhibit Mode Two Behavior are reasonably confident, and possess a fairly high degree of

37

self-esteem. They are usually intelligent, social, and have a decent set of morals and values, as well as a pretty good sense of humor.

WHY MODE TWO BEHAVIOR IS GENERALLY <u>EFFECTIVE</u>

When analyzing the "proactive" component of your behavior ... the "how you behave towards women" aspect ... Mode Two Behavior is reasonably effective. On the positive side, it is very hard to provoke any woman to become angry with you when you exhibit a Mode Two attitude and demeanor. Most women enjoy being around men who are a combination of entertaining, well-mannered, easy to get along with, and non-argumentative. More than likely, you won't do or say anything that will significantly challenge or frustrate a woman's ego. Therefore, it is inevitable that you will be *liked* by most women you acquaint yourself with. More often than not, women will want to share your company, converse with you on a regular or semi-regular basis, and will typically make an effort to develop a friendship with you. They will probably tell their girlfriends how "nice" you are, how much of a "gentleman" you are, and how personable you are.

Mode Two Behavior is more desirable, and more effective, than Mode Three Behavior, because you are [eventually] honest about your true needs, desires, interests, and intentions. But on the downside, Mode Two Behavior is usually **NOT as effective** as Mode One Behavior, because you tend to reveal your needs, desires, interests, and intentions in a manner that is **TOO SLOW, TOO CAUTIOUS, and TOO INDIRECT.** You tend to *"beat-around-the-bush"* quite frequently because you're overly concerned with getting women to *like you* and making them feel *highly comfortable* in your presence prior to letting women know your real thoughts, and what you *really* want from them.

WHY MODE TWO BEHAVIOR IS GENERALLY WEAK

Men who exhibit Mode Two Behavior tend to fall into the trap of engaging in too much pleasant and flattering *small talk* prior to letting a woman know what their true needs, desires, interests, and intentions are. This is why I refer to men who exhibit Mode Two Behavior as "The Pleasant Postponers": They generally tend to delay, or *postpone*, revealing to women what their true thoughts and long-term objectives are.

Plain and simply, men who exhibit Mode Two Behavior are guilty of **talking too much.** Television and film actor Ted Danson was asked one time in an interview, "What lessons did you learn about interacting with women while playing fun-loving womanizer 'Sam Malone' on NBC's 'Cheers'?" He replied, "not to talk so much." He went on to say how he heard from many women that *talking too much* is one of the primary forms of behavior that diminishes your sex appeal. As I mentioned in Chapter Two, there is a difference between **talking** and [verbally] **communicating.**

SOME CLASSIC MODE TWO SCENARIOS

One classic example of exhibiting Mode Two Behavior would be meeting a woman at a social gathering, and proceeding to engage in lighthearted 'chit chat' for a half hour, an hour, or longer. Then, at the *very end of the conversation*, you say something like, "you know what? I think we should get together sometime and go out dancing..." Of course, there's a very good chance that she will reply, *"[Your name], I think you're a very NICE GUY ... but I'm not really interested in you in 'that way'..."* CRUSHED!! Translation: She has all of the platonic interest in you that you could possibly want, but she has very little, if any, romantic and/or sexual interest in you.

Another example would be, you meet a woman . . . ask for her phone number . . . invite her out on a dinner-movie date . . . talk to her a few times over the phone . . . go out on another dinner-movie or dinner-concert date . . . and then . . . FINALLY . . . you communicate to her that "I'm attracted to you, and interested in spending more time with you..." Everything is going fine, right? **WRONG.** After a moment's hesitation, she ends up telling you something along the lines of, *"[Your name], I've had a very, very good time hanging out with you ... I think you're a very NICE GUY ... but my ex-boyfriend 'Chip' (or Roscoe, or Biff, etc.) and I are getting back together very, very soon..."* How do you feel? (okay, dumb question) You are TICKED OFF. You're ANGRY. FRUSTRATED. Even BITTER. You spent all that *time* ...

all that *money* … expressed all that *flattery* … engaged in all of those entertaining *small talk* conversations … and what's your reward? **Another good, platonic female friend.** Poor guy.

Mode Two Behavior is **EFFECTIVE** because, usually, you tend to communicate why you really want to share a woman's company; You're reasonably honest when it comes to conveying your true needs, desires, interests, and long-term intentions to a woman. When it comes to the "proactive" component of your behavior, you get a "B+." Your behavior *towards women* is usually conducive to sharing a woman's company for at least a few days, a few weeks, if not more.

The problem lies in the "responsive" component of your behavior. In other words, when it comes to how you *allow women to behave towards you*, you get anywhere from a C- to a D. In a nutshell, your behavior is **WEAK**. The primary reason why is that *you're too afraid of harsh, subjective criticism.* You're afraid of being <u>disliked</u> by women. As a consequence, your behavior becomes a combination of *too lenient* and *too accommodating.*

Your behavior is too lenient because you do not force a woman to be specific and straightforward in regard to **her** needs, desires, interests, and intentions towards interacting with you. When you exhibit Mode Two Behavior, one of the mistakes you make is that you allow women

41

to remain *too vague* and *ambiguous* in respect to expressing their true thoughts with you. You never want a woman to operate in what I refer to as the **"ambiguous zone."** When you do, platonic friendship is usually the best you can hope for.

Similarly, you can never allow yourself to become too accommodating. What you're guilty of is known as **acquiescent** behavior. Acquiescence means to basically become passive and submissive towards someone in a quiet, subtle manner. Remember the example I used in the previous chapter regarding personal principles and the use of drugs? This relates to the idea of being 'too accommodating.' Generally speaking, any time you violate one or more of your own personal principles and values for the sole and specific purpose of gaining a woman's attention and interest, you're being too accommodating.

This brings me to the whole "he's 'too nice'" syndrome. How many times have you, or a buddy of yours, had the unfortunate (and frustrating) experience of having a woman tell one of her good friends, "I thought he was handsome ... fun to be around ... but he was just 'too nice.'" When I was younger, I can name at least a dozen times when I had a woman lose interest in me because they perceived me as being 'too nice.'

What those women were really saying was that my behavior was too lenient and too accommodating. My behavior was not firm enough, or demanding enough. Even more specifically, my behavior was not **provocative** enough. Most dictionaries define 'provocative' as "arousing, or likely to arouse anger, interest, curiosity, or sexual desire." If you want to have anything beyond a platonic friendship with a female, something about your conversations and interactions with women has to be, to some degree, *provocative.*

THE MISTAKEN BELIEF MOST "NICE GUYS" HAVE

Men, I'm going to tell you a little 'secret' regarding your ability to generate interest from a woman: You are more likely to generate romantic and/or sexual interest from a woman by exhibiting behavior that is *challenging and/or frustrating* to her ego, than you will by exhibiting behavior that is *pleasing and/or flattering* to her ego. In order for there to be any romantic or sexual interest between a male and female, there has to be some degree of **erotic tension.**

When you become interested in watching a good, dramatic television show, soap opera, or movie, it's usually because there's a high degree of **tension** in the story. **No tension, no interest.** I'm a screenwriter, and every workshop I've ever attended, or book I've read, emphasizes that there must be some degree of **tension** and/or conflict incorporated into the story in order for it to be interesting. Believe it or not, it's the same for maintaining interest in a male-female relationship.

Most people look at tension as a 'bad' thing to have in a relationship. **NOT TRUE.** Many men and women **confuse tension with animosity.** These two terms are not the same thing. Animosity between a man and a woman is caused by expressing feelings of hatred or hostility; when your behavior is adversarial or antagonistic. **Tension** in a relationship on the other hand, is caused by feelings of **intrigue, excitement,** or **suspense.** More specifically, 'erotic tension' is the direct result of *provocative behavior* combined with *a certain degree of egotistical frustration.* **Erotic tension is almost a prerequisite for the development of romantic and sexual interest.** This is an important point to remember.

In a matter of speaking, this is what causes most men to become "horny." Most guys think you become horny when you're looking at a porno movie, haven't had sex in a while, or share the company of a woman dressed in a sexy outfit. Those are all factors that *contribute* to a feeling of horniness, but realistically, that's not what really makes you horny (i.e. erotically aroused). Anytime a woman does something or says something that ignites **erotic tension**, you're going to become horny. Again, erotic tension comes from **provocative behavior.** Provocative behavior comes from exhibiting behavior that does not

44

'spoil' or over-flatter a woman's ego. Anytime you're exhibiting behavior that is too pleasing, flattering, and/or accommodating to a woman's ego, then your behavior fails to be provocative. **You cannot create erotic tension without provocative behavior.**

WHAT DOES EROTIC TENSION HAVE TO DO WITH COMMUNICATING?

Now I know many of you might be saying "What does developing erotic tension have to do with my verbal communication skills?" When it comes to attracting women's interest, EVERYTHING. When your behavior is not provocative, you're going to have an exceptionally hard time attracting and maintaining the romantic and sexual interest of a woman. When your behavior is **weak,** it's not provocative. **When your behavior is not provocative, women are going to generally view you as nothing more than a platonic friend.**

When it comes down to the nitty-gritty, the primary reason why most single men exhibit behavior that is 'too nice,' or very basic and conventional towards single women is because **they're afraid of revealing their sexuality to women too quickly.** Just about all men who exhibit Mode Two Behavior are men who are dreadfully afraid of being labeled as 'promiscuous,' 'kinky,' 'horny,' 'shallow,' and/or 'superficial.' I can pretty much guarantee you that if you hypnotized any single man to always be open and honest about his sexual interests, there would be no such thing as Mode Two Behavior.

The reality is **ALL HUMAN BEINGS ARE SEXUAL BEINGS.** If you're a biological creature, you have a sexual nature to you. There is nothing wrong or 'shameful' about having a desire to have sex with a woman. Dr. Blanton, in _Radical Honesty_ makes a statement that "The problem with denying sexual energy is that, sooner or later, somehow or other, it has to be dealt with." I know from taking a human sexuality class in college that most men who become "sexual perverts" are not men who always talk about sex in an open and honest manner. It's JUST THE OPPOSITE. Most men who are perceived as 'perverts' are men who were conditioned to believe that sexual desire was associated with being a 'bad,' 'naughty' person. They associate sex with immorality.

This is what causes that whole "he's 'too nice'" syndrome. In the same way there are men who are guilty of 'overemphasizing' sex, there are men who are guilty of 'underemphasizing' sex. Now don't get me wrong. I'm not saying that every man should approach women and immediately invite them to have sex on the <u>first</u> <u>date</u>. Most women won't go for that. But at the same time, don't go out of your way to suppress (or repress) your sexual energy and interests either. If I had to think of all of the women who I've met, who were initially interested in me, but days or weeks later, lost interest in me, it was typically those women who I 'underemphasized' my sexual desires and interests with. I would say probably 95-99% of the women who labeled me as 'too nice' in the past were women who I very rarely, if ever, discussed anything related to sex with.

Most men who exhibit Mode Two Behavior are generally those men who are afraid to bring the subject of *sex* and *physical romance* into the conversation too quickly or too frequently. **Mode Two men are typically those who always want to make a "good impression" on a female; They always want to present themselves as a 'good, wholesome, monogamous-minded gentleman.'**

Just about every man I've talked to who frequently exhibited Mode Two Behavior, but was afraid to exhibit Mode One Behavior, it was usually because of a fear of being labeled as shallow, superficial, kinky, promiscuous, or "too sexually forward." *Just about all men who exhibit Mode Two Behavior ... deep down ... want to exhibit Mode One Behavior.* But they're too afraid of risking their reputation as a "wholesome, well-mannered gentleman."

If you notice, most males who really don't care about having a wholesome, "gentleman-oriented" reputation, tend to **NATURALLY** exhibit Mode One Behavior. Eddie Murphy, when he first gained popularity, was like that. He was naturally *bold*, extremely *confident*, and *unapologetically straightforward*. He didn't really care if people perceived him as "wholesome" or "well-mannered."

THE "DR. JEKYLL & MR. HYDE" SYNDROME

I can almost guarantee you that anytime you have a 'bad' experience with a woman after exhibiting Mode Two Behavior, you're going to **SWITCH** (either temporarily, or indefinitely) **to a MODE FOUR STATE OF MIND.** It's inevitable. *That's the big weakness in Mode Two Behavior.* Anytime you exhibit Mode Two Behavior, you'll remain happy and content as long as you're NOT being unfairly or harshly criticized, or not feeling disliked or unpopular with women.

Mode Two men can handle being rejected in a nice, considerate manner (e.g., "I'm sorry ... you're a really nice, sweet guy. A perfect gentleman. I just don't think we have any romantic chemistry. You understand, don't you?"). They can even handle being ignored after the rejection, as long as they know that their reputation and image as a gentleman is still in tact. However, as soon as a woman says anything or does anything to threaten their wholesome, "good guy" reputation, or they take advantage of their leniency and overly accommodating behavior, it's *"MODE FOUR, here I come..."*

Another problem with Mode Two Behavior, is that it is **inherently MANIPULATIVE.** Most Mode Two men don't CONSCIOUSLY or INTENTIONALLY set out to manipulate women, but that's what Mode Two Behavior really is: It's manipulative in a subtle, indirect manner. You'll recall from the previous chapter the two types of manipulative behavior that men exhibit: Offering tangible and intangible *incentives and rewards* in exchange for romantic and sexual companionship, <u>OR</u> exhibiting *deceptive, misleading behavior* in order to provoke a specific response.

When you exhibit Mode Two Behavior, you're basically using pleasant, flattering behavior as an *incentive* to motivate the response you want from a woman. Subconsciously, what you're saying to her is "if I behave in a manner that's pleasing to you, I would hope that you would return the favor and eventually behave in a manner that is pleasing to me." *I scratch your back, you scratch mine.* Whether you agree with it or not, when you exhibit Mode Two Behavior, **YOU'RE BEING MANIPULATIVE.**

Again, I don't think most Mode Two men are CONSCIOUSLY or INTENTIONALLY manipulative, but when it's all said and done, Mode Two Behavior is manipulative. Let's be honest: **NO MAN IS AS GENUINELY WELL-MANNERED, or "WHOLESOME," AS THEY <u>PRETEND</u> <u>TO</u> <u>BE</u> TOWARDS A NEW FEMALE ACQUAINTANCE. NO MAN.** I will stand firm behind that opinion.

Most men, particularly those whose mothers had a major influence on how they're "supposed to behave" towards women, tend to behave in a much more pleasant and flattering manner towards women in their *early interactions* with them. How many times have you heard a woman say *"he was so nice to me when he first started pursuing my interest, but once we started dating, HE CHANGED...."* No he didn't. **He didn't change. HE FINALLY CHOSE TO REVEAL WHO HE REALLY WAS IN THE FIRST PLACE.** Essentially, that's all Mode Two is: You're *postponing* revealing to a woman your true desires, interests, intentions, and character. Once you know that a woman is definitely interested in sharing your company in a romantic and/or sexual manner, that's when you tend to reveal **WHO YOU REALLY ARE.**

I once a had a masseuse tell me that "Your 'real' self is synonymous with your sexual self." I would generally agree with that. Look in the dictionary for the formal definition of "sexual." Most men would think to be 'sexual' means to make an effort to have sex with a woman. **NOT TRUE.** That's more so the definition of 'sensual.' The primary definition of being 'sexual' means "of or relating to the sexes (males and females), or the expression of feelings between them" (Oxford American Dictionary). In other words, anytime you're expressing your true thoughts and feelings to a woman, you're being **SEXUAL** (again, not to be confused with "sensual").

I remember when I would engage in sexually provocative conversations with women, some of them would call me "mannish" ("Oh Alan … you're so mannish!") I always thought that to be 'mannish' meant to be 'kinky' or 'erotically naughty.' Look in your dictionary: **To be 'mannish' means to "behave like a man."** While you're examining the dictionary, look up the term "nice." You know what it really means to be 'nice'?? The Latin derivation of "nice" (*nescius*) means to be **ignorant** and **foolish.** The Middle English derivation of "nice" means to be **strange** and **lazy** (Oxford American College dictionary). So, when you're attempting to be a Mode Two "nice guy," you're exhibiting behavior that is strange, lazy, ignorant, and foolish. Surprised?

RECAP

• **When you exhibit Mode Two Behavior, your behavior is generally <u>effective</u>, but <u>weak</u>. It is <u>effective</u> because you're usually honest with women *eventually* about what your true needs, desires, interests, and intentions are, but your behavior is <u>weak</u> because your behavior is too lenient and too accommodating.**

• **When you exhibit Mode Two Behavior, you tend to be deeply afraid of developing a 'negative' or 'controversial' reputation among women; More specifically, you're afraid of engaging in any conversation or discussion that is related to your sexual desires, interests, and intentions. Consequently, your behavior fails to create erotic tension, and you tend to be perceived as 'too nice' by women (i.e., your behavior is not provocative).**

• There is an indirect, if not direct, correlation between a man's level of honesty and sincerity with women, and his lack of fear of being criticized by women. Mode Two men are honest with women only when they're confident that it will provoke a positive, enthusiastic response from women. Mode Two men will be 'pleasantly phony' (i.e., "nice") with women if they think it will prevent and/or avoid harsh, subjective criticism.

• Mode Two men are nicknamed "The Pleasant Postponers" because they tend to delay, or postpone, letting women know what their true romantic and/or sexual needs, desires, interests, and intentions are; Mode Two men are specifically afraid of being perceived as "shallow," "superficial," "kinky," "promiscuous," and/or too sexually "forward." As a result, they will usually wait until a woman perceives them as a "gentleman" before they express their what they're REALLY thinking

• Anytime you exhibit Mode Two Behavior, and you end up getting criticized or disrespected by a woman, your behavior is going to either temporarily or indefinitely switch to Mode Four Behavior. You will be perceived as having a "Dr. Jekyll & Mr. Hyde" personality. You will flip flop back and forth between "nice" behavior and "mean" behavior with women.

When I was younger, and more naive, I used to believe that a woman's *compliments* about my personality and behavior were <u>synonymous</u> with *her interest in me.* I used to really believe that if a woman had a dozen good things to say about me, that this meant that this woman was highly interested in me romantically and/or sexually. Every now and then, that was true, but more often than not, *a woman's compliments were not an accurate indicator of that woman's romantic or sexual interest in me.*

One thing is for sure: **MOST PEOPLE IN GENERAL ARE GOING TO "LIKE YOU" AND SAY "GOOD THINGS" ABOUT YOU WHEN YOU'RE BEING VERY PLEASANT, FLATTERING, AND ACCOMMODATING TOWARDS THEM.** Why wouldn't they? When you're exhibiting Mode Two Behavior, highly manipulative women can easily take advantage of your time, your flattery, and many times, your money.

There's really only one thing worse than exhibiting behavior that allows women to be phony, misleading, and manipulative towards you ... and that's to exhibit behavior in which YOU'RE BEING PHONY, DECEPTIVE, MISLEADING, and MANIPULATIVE TOWARDS THEM. With Mode Two, there's the high potential TO BE MISLED, but **when you exhibit Mode Three Behavior, you're consciously attempting to MISLEAD THEM.**

Again, take out a pencil, and a piece of paper, and think about all of your "beliefs" associated with being perceived as "nice guy."

1)   When you behaved like a "nice guy" (i.e., you were 'well-mannered, and went out of your way to avoid talking about anything erotic with a woman) with women, were your conversations with women always honest and sincere??

2)   How do you generally respond to or react to subjective criticisms??   Do you get egotistically sensitive??   Do you begin to resent the woman who is criticizing you??

3) How many times have you given a woman the impression that she was the only woman you knew in which you were interested in dating and/or having sex with, when you knew that wasn't the truth??   How many times have you been dishonest and/or insincere with a woman in order to maintain a 'wholesome' or 'monogamous' image??

Once you answer these three questions, you're free to proceed to Chapter Four.

CHAPTER FOUR

The Men who Exhibit Mode THREE Behavior: The "Phony Pretenders"

"We lie to avoid whatever we perceive as dangerous – to our ego, to our comfort, to our safety. Most of us lie because our sense of safety and self-esteem depends on our feeling in control, in control of how other people react to us, of whether we appear smart or foolish, of whether we'll get what we want."
Dr. Susan Campbell, author of Getting Real: 10 Truth Skills You Need To Live An Authentic Life

Mode Three Behavior. I would have to say, that out of all the four modes of verbal communication, Mode Three is probably the most pathetic. At least when you exhibit Mode Two Behavior, you're usually confident enough to approach a woman. You just don't have the guts to really be yourself, and express your needs, desires, interests, and intentions in an upfront, straight-to-the-point manner. Many times, when you're in a Mode Three frame of mind, you're usually ***too timid to even APPROACH A WOMAN.*** Fear rides you like a horse. Just about everything about you is fear-based, and consequently, **phony** and **wimpy**. Mode Three Behavior is both **weak** <u>AND</u> **ineffective**.

WHY MODE THREE BEHAVIOR IS <u>INEFFECTIVE</u>

Most men who exhibit Mode Three Behavior generally have a less-than-average degree of self-confidence and self-esteem. They are often perceived as either "shy," "introverted," excessively flattering, indecisive, "wishy washy," and/or generally dishonest. Why?

When I was in my early twenties, my brother Stephen told me "never allow yourself to want a woman 'too badly'." At the time he gave me that piece of advice, I didn't really fully comprehend the meaning of it. As time passed though, and I became wiser and more mature, I began to understand what was meant by his statement.

To want a woman's attention and companionship 'too badly' means you're willing to do practically ANYTHING to gain and maintain a woman's interest. In the long-run, that is not a good thing. When you're willing to compromise your personal principles and values, or worse, sacrifice your sense of dignity and self-respect, for the sake of attracting a woman's interest, this would be representative of wanting a woman's attention and companionship 'too badly.'

This is the primary cause of Mode Three Behavior. When you want to attract a woman's interest 'too badly,' you tend to become more afraid of being rejected and/or ignored by that female. Consequently, the more afraid you are of being rejected or ignored, the more likely you are to exhibit behavior that will prevent and avoid such responses. And ultimately, this is what corrupts and weakens your character.

There are actually *two sub-categories* of Mode Three men: On one end, you have what I will call *"The Timids"*; "Timids" are those Mode Three men who have **NO BALLS**. They have so little confidence in their social skills with women, and such a low degree of courage, that they very rarely, if ever, even attempt to approach a woman. **"Timids" are DREADFULLY AFRAID of rejection.** Another sub-group of Mode Three men would be *"The Targets"*; "Targets" are basically Mode Three men with *money, material possessions, and social connections.* Manipulative women who are gold diggers **love** "Targets." A "Target" is the type of guy who will buy women expensive gifts on a regular basis, pay their rent, finance their education, and anything else that money can buy. **"Targets" never ATTRACT COMPANIONSHIP ... they simply BUY IT.**

TIMIDS

"Timids" are usually men who were probably considered "nerds" or "geeks" in high school and/or college. Their perception of THEMSELVES is so poor, and so weak, to the point that they really don't look at themselves as being romantically or sexually desirable in any way to women. Therefore, they just take themselves off of the playing field completely. They shy away from even conversing or interacting with women. The only women with whom they will halfway interact with, are those women who basically *approach them first*, and express some sort of romantic and/or sexual interest in them *first*. Even then, they tend to harbor a "why would this woman be interested in ME?" attitude. Poor guys.

TARGETS

"Targets" are nothing more than *former "Timids"* who now have achieved a high degree of career success and financial success. A **"Target" is nothing more than a Mode Three Loser with money.** They don't have the confidence to approach women, and attract women, with their looks, intelligence, or personal charm. Instead, they use things like a nice, expensive luxury car, or a big expensive house in order to attract a woman's attention. Two thirds or more of their conversations with women will usually center around **WHAT THEY OWN, HOW MUCH MONEY THEY MAKE, and/or WHAT THEY'VE ACCOMPLISHED CAREER-WISE.**

If you see a guy at a restaurant with three beautiful women at the table with him, don't be too quick to say "Oh ... he must've used Mode One Behavior!" Not necessarily. A Mode Three man could know a lot of women, and even go out on dates with a lot of women, but it comes at a *steep price.* Many times, a Mode Three man will spend hundreds, if not thousands of dollars on *women who he is not even dating or having sex with.* They just want "the appearance" of being popular with women.

Mode Three men are notorious for excessive and/or insincere flattery, expensive wining & dining, going out of their way to impress women, and even many times, exhibiting submissive and deferential behavior towards women. **Mode Three men have a VERY LOW degree of self-confidence and self-esteem.** It would not be uncommon for a Mode Three man to start a conversation by saying, *"You know I have an MBA from Harvard don't you..."*

SOME CLASSIC MODE THREE SCENARIOS

One classic example of exhibiting Mode Three Behavior as a "Timid" (i.e., a Mode Three Loser with absolutely no courage) would be attending a social function that you were invited to, and then proceeding to play the role of "wallflower." You see a number of women with whom you find physically attractive, but at no time during this social function do you make an attempt to introduce yourself to any of these desirable females. *Your shyness, which is the result of your fears, insecurities, and low self-esteem, paralyzes you from taking action.* Poor guy.

If you're exhibiting Mode Three Behavior as a "Target" (i.e., a Mode Three Loser with money and social status), you would probably muster up enough courage to at least *talk* to women you're interested in, but you would immediately let it be known that you "don't want anything from them." Just about your whole conversation with women would revolve around *pretentious, uninteresting small talk.* You would never even **dare** express your romantic and/or sexual desires, interests, and intentions to a woman in an honest, upfront, straight-to-the-point manner. You wouldn't even express your interests in a *roundabout* manner. You will simply *hide* or *camouflage* what your true interests are, *unless that female expresses similar interests first.* Otherwise, you will highlight everything you've accomplished and achieved in your life throughout your conversation with women, in an attempt to **impress them**. If you're at a bar or restaurant, you will immediately *offer to pay* for the women's drinks and food. Soon, if they take the bait, you will be 'wining & dining' one or more of these women for days, weeks, or months.

I actually would blame Mode Three men, and "Targets" in particular, on why there are so many spoiled, highly manipulative gold diggers in society. Because they have no real confidence, they use their *finances* and *material possessions* as their #1 source of confidence and self-esteem. **"Targets" have what's known as <u>false</u> <u>confidence</u>.** And consequently, gold digging, manipulative women become accustomed to having their way with these types of men. When you exhibit Mode Three Behavior, you can be very easily manipulated, if not flat out **dominated**, by women.

Mode Three Behavior is almost totally predicated on <u>FEAR</u>. And like I pointed out in previous chapters, there is a direct correlation between how fearful you are, and how manipulative you are. The more afraid you are of straightforwardly expressing to people what it is you want from them, the more likely you are to attempt to manipulate them in order to get it. No one represents this more than a man who exhibits Mode Three Behavior.

The primary reason why Mode Three men can be so easily manipulated is because THEY ARE TRYING TO MANIPULATE WOMEN THEMSELVES. Like I said in Chapter Two: *MANIPULATION IS ALWAYS A TWO-WAY STREET.* **The more you attempt to manipulate someone, the more you open yourself up to BE MANIPULATED.** Whereas a Mode Two man will simply *postpone* expressing his true desires and intentions, a Mode Three man will *indefinitely HIDE them, DENY them, or CAMOUFLAGE them.* He doesn't want his true desires and intentions being known, because *he's too afraid that they won't be reciprocated.*

"Timids" are deeply afraid of being rejected; "Targets" are deeply afraid of being ignored. Anytime you allow yourself to become highly afraid of either one, you will find yourself exhibiting Mode Three Behavior. You will generally come across to women as *phony, wimpy, hypocritical, two-faced, sneaky, conniving, manipulative, and insincerely flattering.* Women basically despise you and/or feel sorry for you, but again, if you have wealth, status, and material possessions, they will **pretend** as though they are interested in you.

Mode Three Behavior is **INEFFECTIVE** because you're willing to exhibit deceitful and/or manipulative behavior in order to secure a woman's attention and companionship. If you're really interested in a short-term, casual sex relationship, you will "pretend" as though you're interested in a long-term, serious romantic relationship. If you're really interested in a romantic relationship, you will "pretend" as though you're totally content with just a good, platonic friendship. Why? **Because you're afraid that whatever your interests are, they won't be reciprocated.** That's why I refer to men who exhibit Mode Three Behavior as the "Phony Pretenders."

WHY MODE THREE BEHAVIOR IS WEAK

To compound the criticisms of why Mode Three Behavior is ineffective towards accomplishing your objectives, it is also **weak** in regard to how you allow women to behave towards you. In the previous chapter, I said that a man exhibiting Mode Two Behavior would receive a letter grade that is anywhere from a "C- to a D." For those who exhibit Mode Three Behavior, you would probably receive a D- or an F. Because of your deep, profound **fear of being rejected and/or ignored**, you will do practically ANYTHING to maintain a woman's attention and companionship, including allowing yourself to be treated in a highly undesirable, disrespectful manner.

Earlier in this chapter, I talked about the concept of wanting a woman's attention 'too badly.' How many times have you heard one or more of your male friends say something along the lines of, "I would do *anything* to date her!" or "I would give *anything* to have sex with her just one time!" Once you allow yourself to adopt attitudes such as these, you're setting yourself up to become a **loser** with women.

It's actually these very attitudes that cause anger, egotistical frustration, and misogynistic bitterness later on. The reason being is that anytime you're willing to violate one or more of your personal principles and values for the sake of attracting a woman's attention, or worse, you're willing to allow yourself to be disrespected and treated like crap in order to gain some measure of attention from a woman, at some point your ego is going to kick in. First regret sets in, then frustration, then anger.

Write this down so you can remember it, and repeat it to yourself:

NO WOMAN'S ATTENTION or COMPANIONSHIP IS WORTH SACRIFICING YOUR SENSE OF DIGNITY, PERSONAL HONOR, or SELF-RESPECT FOR.

Did you see the movie *Braveheart*? Mel Gibson's character, Scottish warrior William Wallace, was willing to die . . . **DIE** . . . rather than compromise his principles and values, or sacrifice his sense of dignity, personal honor, and self-respect. Think about that. This guy was willing to sacrifice his **LIFE**, rather than allow himself to be treated like a disrespected, subservient slave. This is the problem with most, if not all men, who exhibit Mode Three Behavior on a regular basis. Your behavior is *obsequious*. Obsequious means that you're *too anxious* and *overeager* to please someone, serve someone, and/or obey someone. A Mode Three man tends to *fawn* over women (i.e., you attempt to attract attention from women, and favor from women, by excessively playing up to their egos). **THIS IS WHY MODE THREE BEHAVIOR IS WEAK.** Even 'weaker' than Mode Two Behavior.

Right now, I'm going to take the time to address a common misperception of Mode One Behavior. There have been some women, who've read my original manuscript, that made the comment that "Alan, it sounds as if you're against men flattering women, or just being platonic friends with women." **THIS IS NOT TRUE.** I have nothing against a man expressing an occasional compliment, or maintaining a platonic relationship with a woman, *if it's mutual and reciprocated.* I do not believe in 'non-reciprocal' flattery. Anytime you're constantly playing up to a woman's ego, but that same woman very rarely, if ever, flatters your ego, that is what's referred to (in urban slang) as "jocking" a woman. Similarly, **I'm against men PRETENDING to be content with just a "platonic" friendship, when they know deep down that they want more than that.** That's the biggest scheme of a Mode Three man (Timids and Targets): *They will usually indefinitely PRETEND as* *though they're happy "just being your friend," but* **in reality, they are** *dying to date you, or have sex with you.* **BUT THEY DON'T HAVE THE BALLS TO TELL YOU.**

Like I said, even though I have some major criticisms of Mode Four Behavior, I think exhibiting Mode Three Behavior is WORSE. **Mode Three is the worst of the four modes.** Everything about you is **NOT REAL.** You're not honest, you're not straightforward, you're not confident, and you're not trustworthy. **You are a TOTAL VERBAL WIMP.**

HOW INVALID BELIEFS LEAD TO EGOTISTICAL INSECURITY

The biggest obstacle that Mode Three men have to overcome is **egotistical insecurity.** What is it that actually causes egotistical insecurity? I would say the starting point, or core, of all egotistical insecurities is **invalid beliefs** and/or **false assumptions.** More specifically, you have a misconception about what is desirable to women, and what is not. First of all though, what is an insecurity?

An insecurity is **a perception within your own mind** that an attribute or characteristic you possess is not quite "up to par," so to speak. For example, if it is your belief that all women are attracted to men who are six feet tall, or taller, then you're going to become insecure if you stand at a height of 5'8". If it is your belief that a high salary is the #1 thing that attracts the interest of a woman, then you're going to feel insecure anytime you're in the company of another man who is earning more money than you.

The key to remember is that **all insecurities begin, and end, in your own mind**. Now if a woman specifically informs you herself of her particular tastes and preferences in men, all you can do is accept them, and if you don't fit the bill, move on. If a woman says "I only like men who drive European cars," and you're driving an American car, what can you do? Realistically though, most men make **assumptions** about what women find desirable, and what they don't find desirable.

Anytime you 'compare' what you have to offer women, with what other men have to offer women, you're setting yourself up to develop a number of egotistical insecurities. This is why you should never base your sense of self-confidence and self-esteem on one specific thing. For example, if 90% of your self-esteem is based on your looks, guess what's going to happen if you're in the company of another man who you perceive as more handsome than you? You're going to feel very **insecure.** Same thing goes for your level of wealth, your sense of humor, your level of education, your degree of career success, and so on and so on. Your confidence and self-esteem has to come from your "total package." Every quality about you **combined together** should be the basis for your sense of confidence and self-esteem, not just one particular attribute.

RECAP

• **When you exhibit Mode Three Behavior, your behavior is generally <u>weak</u> AND <u>ineffective</u>. It is <u>weak</u> because you're willing to do *anything* to attract and maintain the interest of a woman, even if it means allowing yourself to be used, manipulated, or disrespected. It is <u>ineffective</u> because you typically hide, deny, and/or camouflage your true needs, desires, interests, and intentions from a woman, primarily because you're afraid that they won't be satisfied and reciprocated.**

• **When you exhibit Mode Three Behavior, you tend to be deeply afraid of being rejected and/or ignored. Those Mode Three men who are more so afraid of rejection are known as "Timids"; These men very rarely, if ever, will even muster up enough courage to even approach a woman. Those Mode Three men who are more so afraid of being ignored are known as "Targets"; These men use their accomplishments and material possessions as the primary basis for their conversations with women.**

• **"Targets" will typically share the company of attractive, desirable women, but not those who have a genuine interest in them.**

"Targets" usually attract manipulative, materialistic women who are only interested in taking advantage of a man's money, material possessions, and social connections.

• Mode Three men are nicknamed "The Phony Pretenders" because they will frequently 'pretend' to have a platonic interest in a woman, when deep down, their interest is romantic and/or sexual.

• Anytime you exhibit Mode Three Behavior, it's primarily because you're <u>egotistically insecure</u>. Egotistical insecurities are usually the result of invalid beliefs and assumptions that you have developed over the years. Insecurities result from what you <u>assume</u> is desirable and undesirable to women. When you base your self-confidence and self-esteem on one particular characteristic or attribute, you're more likely to become insecure.

Mode Three Behavior should be avoided as much as possible. **Women don't respect men who exhibit Mode Three Behavior, and other men don't respect men who exhibit Mode Three Behavior.** Don't allow yourself to become a woman's monetary play toy!! If you're a "Timid" ... take inventory of what you have to offer, and **GROW SOME BALLS.** If you're a "Target," quit trying to impress women with your level of wealth and/or material possessions in an attempt to "purchase" their companionship. **THAT IS WEAK.** You look pathetic and desperate.

"What if I've been dumped on after using Mode Two AND Mode Three?? What if I've been taken advantage of so many times by women, that I have nothing but hurt feelings and bitter resentment?? What's that called when you feel horrible like I do???"

That's called **Mode Four** Behavior. **Uh oh.** Before you proceed to Chapter Five, please honestly answer the following questions:

1) What characteristic about yourself makes you feel the most confident and egotistically secure? (e.g., your looks, your intelligence, your career status, etc.) On the flip side, what characteristic do you possess that you <u>perceive</u> as being undesirable to women?? Did you assume this, or did women specifically tell you that this attribute was undesirable to them??

2) Think of one or more women from your past that you "pretended" to have nothing more than a platonic interest in, but deep down, you had a romantic and/or sexual interest in them. What most prevented you from revealing your true feelings?

3) How many times have you conversed with a woman, and primarily emphasized your educational and career accomplishments and/or your financial status and materialistic possessions in order to increase a woman's interest in you?? Why did you feel it was necessary to do this??

Once you answer these three questions, you're free to proceed to Chapter Five.

CHAPTER FIVE

The Men who Exhibit Mode FOUR Behavior: The "Misogynistic Revenge Seekers"

"Look at the weaknesses of others with compassion, not accusation. It's not what they're not doing or should be doing that's the issue. The issue is your own chosen response to the situation and what you should be doing. If you start to think the problem is 'out there,' stop yourself. That thought is the problem."
Dr. Steven R. Covey, author of <u>The Seven Habits of Highly Effective People</u>

Mode Four Behavior. Well, well, well. You met some women, and you were too quickly impressed with their looks, intelligence, level of education, and/or degree of career success, so you found yourself exhibiting Mode Two Behavior. Eventually, you got *treated like a platonic friend*, and when you tried to be more romantic or sexual, you got <u>CRITICIZED</u>. Or, you met some women, and you were too easily intimidated by those same qualities, and you found yourself exhibiting Mode Three Behavior. And you got *used*, *dominated*, *manipulated*, and then <u>IGNORED</u>. **Now you are TICKED OFF.**

When a man finds himself in a state of mind where he is seething with anger, engulfed with bitterness, and overflowing with

egotistical frustration, there's only one remedy he can think of: MODE FOUR BEHAVIOR. "Dr. Jekyll" turns into "Mr. Hyde," and *the dark side is unleashed* (think about any serial killer who targets women, or any rapist ... Mode Four Behavior at it's worst).

You can almost bet your mortgage that if you see a man exhibiting some variation of Mode Four Behavior towards a woman, *at some point in his past, he either consistently behaved in a Mode Two manner and/or a Mode Three manner.* He wanted a specific, desirable response from a number of females, but failed to get them. Men who exhibit Mode Four Behavior towards women could care less now about actually attracting a woman's romantic or sexual interest. **They're past that point. They want emotional and egotistical REVENGE.** Their feelings of vengeance are <u>DEEP</u>, and can be directed at two or three females in particular, or the whole female gender in general.

WHY MODE FOUR BEHAVIOR IS <u>INEFFECTIVE</u>

Most men who exhibit Mode Four Behavior usually possess a high degree of very misogynistic attitudes towards women. They are still physically and sexually aroused by women, but they do not respect them as human beings. **They literally despise women.** When it comes to interacting with women, they have a "chip on their shoulder."

Unlike Mode Two Behavior, *you don't fear being criticized or disliked*, because you've ALREADY BEEN CRITICIZED and DISLIKED too many times. It doesn't faze you anymore. Now, to a large degree, **YOU WANT TO BE DISLIKED.** You <u>want</u> women harshly criticizing you and calling you insulting names. Similarly, unlike Mode Three Behavior, *you no longer fear being rejected or ignored.* You're to a point now where you almost DARE a woman to reject you. **You practically dare a woman to ignore you.** No more "Mr. Nice Guy" for you. Your specific, motivated purpose for interacting with women is to **HURT THEIR FEELINGS** and **BRUISE THEIR EGOS.** *You now actually GAIN PLEASURE and SATISFACTION from knowing that women can't stand you and bad mouth you to friends.* YOU DON'T GIVE A DAMN ANYMORE.

A CLASSIC MODE FOUR SCENARIO

You invested time, effort, flattery, and small talk pursuing a woman's attention and interest, only to have this same woman inform you on your third date with her that she's getting back with her ex-boyfriend. Matter of fact, you went on three dates and didn't even get a **kiss.** You did your best to move on to the next woman, but similar scenarios unfolded at least four to five more times. **CLASSIC MODE TWO RESULTS.** You're angry … you're bitter.

You lay low socially for two or three months, but it just so happens that you run into one of the women with whom you had a Mode Two dinner-movie date with while shopping in the neighborhood grocery store. Initially, you're reluctant to speak, because your mind is still full of frustration from her treating you like a platonic friend, but because she looks good in that tight, short skirt she's wearing, you go ahead and say something. She feigns as if she doesn't remember you (she does), but eventually utters the classic phony response, *"ohh ... I remember you now...."* **OUCH.**

You two talk about what's been happening in your lives the past two to three months, and she mentions that she now lives just two blocks away from where you currently reside. Like an idiot who's forgotten the past, you ask her for her new number (remember, she already played you like two-day old ground beef once). She replies, *"well ... I don't know ...* (pause) *Why don't you give me YOUR number ..."* <u>You</u>: "I thought you had my number ... you had it before ..." <u>Her</u>: *"That's right. I don't think I have it though.* (she's lying. She has your number ... she just hasn't been motivated to use it. But right now, she's pulling an 'egotistical power play' on you to see if you're going to give up the digits; if you do, she knows she has the egotistical "upper hand" in the manipulative "head games" that you two are engaging in) *Can you give it to me again??"* You think for a moment, and like a desperate idiot, you provide her with your home phone number for the second time in less than four months.

Two weeks have passed. No call. Your sense of desperation for her attention leads you to call her old phone number, and to your surprise, they offer a forwarding number (her new number that she wouldn't offer you in the grocery store). You call. She picks up the phone. As soon as she recognizes your voice, she says *"How did you get my number??"* You say something stupid like, "Oh … I have my ways." Immediately, she tells you that she has her Uncle Chester on the other line *(she's lying … she would never talk to an 'Uncle Chester').*

Three more weeks pass. No call. You call her again and leave an extra long voice mail message explaining that you're not trying to hook up with her for the sake of a "date" or anything romantic. You say *"I JUST WANT TO HANG OUT WITH YOU AS FRIENDS."* **MODE THREE BEHAVIOR AT IT'S BEST** (or worst).

Well, that message might have done the trick. The next day, she calls back, engages you in some entertaining **small talk,** and invites you to a get-together she's having this upcoming weekend. She says, "Since *we're just friends,* I see no reason why you can't come over and hang out…" If you truly just want to be 'just friends' with her, then Jennifer Lopez and Halle Berry have problems attracting men. Yeah, okay. Riiiiiiight..

The weekend comes, you go over to her place, and there's about fifteen to twenty other guests there. You mingle and engage in ... ugh ... **small talk**. You see a guy there who you know from the health club. You guys get to talking, and you mention that you and the host of the party (your 'good buddy'!!) went out on a few dates two to three months ago. Surprisingly, he says, *"I bet she turned you out didn't she!!"* You're stumped. What is he talking about? *"I mean ... that girl is a FREAK. She loves to have sex in every room she possibly can..."* You are in a state of shock. You foolishly confess "Man, ... I didn't even get as much as a kiss..." Your health club buddy *laughs uncontrollably.* *"Are you serious?!?!"* he inquires. You have a look of **frustration** and **embarrassment**. He continues with *"man, I was in bed with her on the FIRST DATE. I know at least three or four other guys that 'tapped that ass'* (i.e., had sex with her) *within a week after they met her..."* Needless to say, the way you're feeling, this is the last thing you needed to hear.

Guess what's starting to fester inside of you? Exactly. **MODE FOUR BEHAVIOR.** You are now on a mission to achieve some emotional and/or egotistical revenge. Instead of leaving the party when the majority of the guests do, you manage to find a way to 'hang around.' Now it's just the host, and one of her girlfriends. Of course, she's like *"are you still here?? the party is pretty much over."* Like you care. She gives you subtle hints that she's ready for you to leave, but you choose to ignore them. Finally, you make up this ridiculous story that your shower is broke, and can you use her shower. She's like *"oh HELL no..."* **BUT** ... to your surprise... her one remaining girlfriend says "oh what the hell! Go ahead and let him use your shower...." So much for small favors.

She reluctantly hands you a towel and a washcloth, and says *"go for it."* You actually pretend as though you really need to take a shower (classic **Mode Three** Behavior).

You take your shower, then get out of the shower, and wrap the towel around your waist. Since you've been working out at the gym, you decide to walk in her living room wearing just the towel. **The host looks at you as if you've lost your DAMN MIND** (but her not-so-attractive friend is smiling flirtatiously at you). The host curiously asks, *"Why are you standing there in just a towel?!?"* Suddenly, you lose all your sense of rational thinking, and **let the towel drop to the ground.** The host immediately jumps up, turns her back to you, and demands that you get your clothes and leave (but her friend stares at your manhood ... too bad she's not your type). The host threatens to call the police if you don't leave within the next five minutes.

Uh oh. "Dr. Jekyll" is about to unleash "Mr. Hyde" ... Mode Four Behavior takes over.

Anger and bitterness overwhelms your emotions, and suddenly you angrily ask, "So what's up with you anyway????" <u>Her</u>: *"What do you mean, 'what's up with me?'* ... *what in the hell is up with YOU?!?"* <u>You</u>: "Why you tryin' to play me??? ... I already know you're a freak ... you've fu**ed every handsome guy you've met ... but you play me like the 'nice guy' chump. What's up with that?!?!"

Now you've done it. She picks up the phone and calls the police. You finally decide to get your clothes and get out of there. But not before you leave her with a few choice words. "Yeah, ... I'll go ahead and leave ... you fu**in' BITCH!!!!" **Mode Four is controlling your behavior, and you've lost it.**

Now you might be reading this, and saying to yourself, "I've never lost it like that. . ." Maybe YOU haven't, but plenty of guys have. I've heard a number of men and women share with me their "Mode Four horror stories." Matter of fact, I know a female friend of mine in Dallas told me about how a neighbor of hers used the "my shower is broken" routine to try to seduce her, because he heard another male neighbor had sex with her fairly quickly.

WHY DOES ANGER & FRUSTRATION CAUSE MODE FOUR BEHAVIOR?

When a man chooses to exhibit Mode Four Behavior towards a woman, he fools himself into believing that he's been mistreated because "all women are bitches!" and "women are nothing but scandalous, untrustworthy whores!" The last woman you interacted with "dogged you," "dissed you," and didn't treat you with any respect. *Realistically, the majority of your anger and frustration is NOT directed at the women in your past.* Deep down, subconsciously, it's directed at **YOURSELF.**

Here's the REAL DEAL: **You are mad at yourself for failing to be your REAL, TRUE SELF from Day One.** That's the REAL issue. You're frustrated that you failed to express your real needs, desires, interests, and intentions in a confident, upfront, and straightforward manner in your first conversation/early interactions with women. You knew when you first met that last female who "took advantage of you" that you wanted to date her, or have casual sex with her. Instead of being provocatively straightforward and upfront, you delayed the process ... and then when you finally did express what was really on your mind, you expressed yourself in an overly cautious, indirect, "beat-around-the-bush" type manner [**Mode Two** Behavior]; Or, even worse, you spent days, weeks, or even months and years <u>PRETENDING</u> that you were content with being "just friends," when all the while you knew that you wanted to exchange pleasurable orgasms with this woman. At some point though, you probably tried to get sexual with her through some sneaky, deceptive, manipulative "scheme," but you failed, and you failed MISERABLY [**Mode Three** Behavior].

Now, you're **ANGRY**.
You're **BITTER**.
You're **EGOTISTICALLY FRUSTRATED**.
You want **REVENGE**.
Shame, shame, shame.

WHY MODE FOUR BEHAVIOR IS <u>STRONG</u>

Despite the fact that Mode Four Behavior is ineffective, Mode Four Behavior is actually representative of 'strong' behavior. When you're exhibiting Mode Four Behavior, no woman can use you, manipulate you, or waste your time. Your anger causes you to become very firm in your personal principles. When you're angry, you don't care about other people's subjective criticisms and opinionated perceptions of you. That's the least thing on your mind. And that's a good thing.

The problem is that you allowed yourself to get to this point in the first place. Mode Four Behavior could have been prevented. THINK ABOUT IT. **Are you beginning to understand who and what is your worst enemy?**

RECAP

• When you exhibit Mode Four Behavior, your behavior is generally <u>strong</u>, but <u>ineffective</u>. It is <u>strong</u> because you're expressing what's really on your mind, and that alone makes it hard for people to manipulate you and/or disrespect you. You're being guided by your own personal principles. It is <u>ineffective</u> because most of what you're expressing is "after-the-fact" information; Because you weren't upfront with your real needs, desires, interests, and intentions, you're now bitter because you know for a fact that they won't be satisfied or reciprocated.

• When you exhibit Mode Four Behavior, your main focus is not on gaining a woman's attention or interest, but rather or gaining some measure of emotional and/or egotistical 'revenge.' Your primary objective is to hurt a woman's feelings, or bruise her ego.

• When you exhibit Mode Four Behavior, you tend to fool yourself into believing that all women are 'no good,' but in reality, their behavior towards you has very little to do with your anger and resentment. Deep down, subconsciously, you're angry at YOURSELF for not being your REAL self. You either temporarily (Mode Two) or indefinitely (Mode Three) expressed thoughts and feelings that were not truly representative of your needs, desires, interests, and intentions, and now you're frustrated that you weren't honest and upfront from Day One.

- **Mode Four men are nicknamed "The Misogynistic Revenge Seekers" because they have reached a point emotionally where they despise and disrespect women.** They are still attracted to women physically and sexually, but they hate women as human beings. They want women to criticize them and hate them back.

In a lot of ways, you can look at Mode Four Behavior as "after-the-fact" Mode One Behavior. Once a woman has *already* criticized you … *already* expressed that she dislikes you … *already* has rejected you … or *already* has blown you off and ignored you … **THEN** … all of the sudden *you get the guts* to express your thoughts, opinions, and objectives in a blunt, straight-to-the-point, unapologetic manner. But by then, it's ineffective, and more importantly ... it's **too late**.

So you now want me to tell you that Mode One Behavior is the "perfect" behavior to exhibit. That all women will automatically *love you, adore you, and desire you* when you exhibit Mode One Behavior … right? **Wrong.** There are some women who actually **DESPISE** the use of Mode One Behavior. "Who?" You guessed it. **HIGHLY MANIPULATIVE WOMEN.**

Before you proceed to Chapter Six though, please honestly answer the following questions:

1) What women from your past left you feeling so angry, frustrated, and bitter that you wanted to do anything possible to make them feel like crap?? (i.e., you wanted some emotional and/or egotistical "revenge")

2) What has generally been your #1 subjective criticism of women in general?? (for example, "They're too materialistic..." or "They're too hypocritical..." or "They're too moody..."; Be as specific as possible.)

3) How many times have you specifically tried to get a woman to 'dislike' you?? Think of at least two or three women who you actually wanted to criticize you or say bad things about you. Why??

Once you answer these three questions, you're free to proceed to Chapter Six.

.

CHAPTER SIX

Casual Sex VS Relationships: "Wholesome Pretenders" and "Erotic Hypocrites"

"Most women love sex just as much as men, if not more. Many women are just as sexually uninhibited as a lot of the kinky men out there. The problem is, men are admired and patted on the back when they successfully seduce a lot of women; Women are usually 'looked down on,' criticized, and made to feel like whores if they reveal that they've enjoyed sexual pleasure with someone other than their boyfriend, fiancé, or husband. It's unfair, but that's life."
A female friend of mine from college

Sex. If men and women were socialized in the exact same manner regarding their attitudes towards sexual relations, our dialogue with each other would probably be a lot more honest, and a lot less manipulative. Men would probably be a lot more honest and straightforward with women regarding their sexual desires and interests, particularly as it relates to their desire for *casual* sex. Then again, there have actually been studies conducted that revealed that men in serious relationships, or even married men, are many times close-mouthed when it comes to expressing their thoughts and desires related to sex. Why?

Nobody likes to be judged. What many men fail to consciously realize is that we indirectly cause women to behave in a manipulative manner towards us when we create these "good girl" vs. "bad girl" distinctions. Most women who aspire to have a high quality, monogamous husband want to be known as a "good girl." The problem is, sometimes their hormones and libidos don't cooperate in assisting them towards maintaining that "wholesome" image and reputation. Many times, we as men tend to possess this hypocritical double-standard that women should be more self-controlled sexually than us. They should be able to resist the temptation of casual, promiscuous sex much easier than us. **Some women can. Others cannot.**

Women know that many men are reluctant to marry a woman who has a history of too many "one-night stands" and/or "casual flings." Some men will meet a woman, try their best to seduce them into having sex as quickly as possible, and if these women resist, they'll leave them alone. They will treat them as though they're 'prudish' or 'boring.' On the other hand, if these same women give in too quickly, they eventually become known as a "ho" or a "freak" among the men's buddies. Some women see this as a no-win situation, so what's their next step? *To lead a "double life." To become __misleading__ and __deceptive__ regarding their sexual behavior, as well as their sexual history.*

You see, men don't share this same pressure to be a "good boy." I know from both experience and observation that a man's level of desirability as a potential husband or boyfriend doesn't suffer nearly as much as a result of some past episodes of kinky, casual, promiscuous sex. I've actually heard men say things like "I'd rather marry a woman who had sex with ten 'ex-boyfriends' than marry a woman who had five 'one-night stands'..." It's these attitudes by men who give birth to two types of manipulative women: *Wholesome Pretenders [WPs] and Erotic Hypocrites [EHs].* These types of women actually _despise_ Mode One Behavior.

WHOLESOME PRETENDERS

A "Wholesome Pretender" [WP] is a type of manipulative female who likes to "have her cake and eat it too." This is a woman who will generally give off the *public* impression that she is innocent, wholesome, virtuous, and all about monogamous relationships. She wants to receive that "I-will-only-have-sex-with-you-within-the-context-of-a-serious-relationship" respectability. These women will have you believing that their middle name is "Chastity." WPs will make a habit out of feigning embarrassment over the mere mention of something sexually raunchy. They will blush when you say the "F" word. They will give you the false impression that their most glaring virtues are their indefinite sense of sexual self-control, their erotic patience and conservatism, and virgin-like prudence.

Most men who exhibit Mode Two Behavior and Mode Three Behavior will typically put these women on a pedestal. In their naivety, they will often times fall for the WP façade. What these men don't consistently realize, is that *a WP's public image is far different than their 'behind-closed-doors' persona.* WPs probably know more sexual positions than the average man. They can express better "dirty pillow talk" than you. They've probably had just as many, if not more, "casual flings" as you have. But they know how to keep their sexual history discreetly *private.*

Why do Wholesome Pretenders despise Mode One Behavior? Because when a man expresses his sexual desires and interests to them in a totally confident, upfront, and unapologetically straight-to-the-point manner, a WP has no choice but to have one of two reactions: **a)** to pretend as though you're 'offending them,' and 'turning them off' *(you're not)* by being so 'forward' with your interests, but then they risk missing out on the opportunity for some sexual companionship they may enjoy; OR **b)** to immediately acknowledge that they have the same exact erotic desires and interests as you do, but then they risk ruining their public reputation as being chaste, wholesome, and sexually prudent. As **manipulative women**, WPs feel like they lose either way. *This is why they don't particularly care for Mode One Behavior.*

How can you usually **identify** a Wholesome Pretender? Anytime you approach a woman, and express a desire to be physically romantic or sexual with them in a Mode One manner, they will typically become very dramatic and theatrical in their response. *"Excuse me??!"* *"I* *don't believe you just said that!!" "Do you talk like this to ALL women??!" "You are SO forward!!"* These are all common responses from your average WP. A key characteristic of WP behavior is that they will usually **subjectively criticize** your manner of expression, but *they will never make an [immediate] attempt to stop interacting with you.* The reason being, is that WPs don't criticize you because your behavior truly "turns them off," but they criticize you in order to give you the [false] impression that they are a "lady," and that "respectable ladies aren't supposed to be talked to in an unapologetically straightforward manner" *(but deep down, they're aroused and/or intrigued by such behavior).*

The biggest thing to remember about WPs is that they *thoroughly enjoy sex . . . even very kinky, casual, highly promiscuous sex, . . . but they also want very badly to avoid being labeled as "sleazy" or a "ho."* They will do **just about anything** to maintain the image and reputation of an "innocent," "wholesome," marriageable woman.

Why do WPs like to play manipulative head games? Because, in a nutshell, they want to 'have their cake and eat it too.' *(Remember: This is the basic motivation for all WPs and EHs)* In a lot of ways, women who are Wholesome Pretenders are very, very similar to **men who exhibit Mode Two Behavior.** A man who frequently exhibits Mode Two Behavior is a man who will postpone expressing his romantic and sexual interests to a woman until he's sure of the fact that a woman 'likes' him, and has a 'favorable impression' of him. **WPs have the same motivations.** A Wholesome Pretender will usually delay revealing their sexual desires and interests to a man, particularly if they revolve around casual sex rather than relationship sex, until they feel as though a man has the utmost of respect for them. WPs will usually make an episode of casual sex seem like it's 'unexpected' or 'spontaneous' *(e.g., "Oh ... I am so drunk! ... I don't really know what I'm doing!" or "you know what? You're the very first guy who I've EVER had sex with on the first date!!" [yeah, right. And she's never seen a porno movie either])* A Wholesome Pretender will never want an episode of casual sex and/or kinky sex to appear "pre-planned" or "well thought of ahead of time." **This would totally ruin the manipulative game that they are trying to play.**

EROTIC HYPOCRITES

"Erotic Hypocrites" [EHs] are very similar to Wholesome Pretenders, only they are much more phony, pretentious, conniving, materialistic, and hypocritical than the average WP. WPs simply want to get married PERIOD. They're not ultra-selective about the type of man they want to marry. EHs on the other hand, tend to have a specific interest in marrying a man with a high degree of wealth and social status. They typically set their sights on men making six figures or higher, who have a high degree of education and/or who come from a prestigious family background. They are status-oriented gold diggers and husband hunters with one particular weakness: *They love raunchy, kinky sex.* EHs usually do a good job of hiding this weakness though.

Most men who exhibit Mode Two Behavior and Mode Three Behavior will typically fall prey to these women. **Mode Three "Targets" in particular will become frequent victims of EHs.** Erotic Hypocrites are the type of women who will criticize men for watching pornographic movies, but will turn around and invite a chosen sexual companion to video tape their episodes of kinky sex. An EH will publicly criticize women for being prostitutes and Call Girls, but they will all but demand that a man wine & dine them prior to having sex with them *(Why is prostitution illegal, yet 'wining & dining' a woman in exchange for sexual companionship legal??).* EHs will usually not marry you because they love having sex with you. They will marry you for your money and social status. Nine times out of ten, they will have **another man on the side** who is creating pleasurable orgasms for them. **EHs love raunchy, kinky sex.** Many times, they even love promiscuous sex with many [discreet] partners. The thing is, if you're a man exhibiting Mode Two Behavior, or worse, a Mode Three "Target," *you'll never find this out.*

Why do Erotic Hypocrites despise Mode One Behavior? Because EHs love to be excessively flattered and wined & dined. **If you're**

90

exhibiting **Mode One Behavior,** *you will never do that.* EHs love to be spoiled with gifts and financial favors. A man exhibiting Mode One Behavior *will never do that.* EHs love to date and marry men more so for their wealth and social status, rather than the fact that they enjoy their company physically and sexually. A man exhibiting Mode One Behavior *will see right through this façade.* For these reasons, among others, EHs get very, very frustrated when they encounter a man who exhibits Mode One Behavior. Deep down, an Erotic Hypocrite knows that a man who has a Mode One attitude and demeanor could probably get them aroused, and seduce them into having sex without offering any type of tangible "incentive" or "reward" in exchange for their sexual companionship. *This is why they don't particularly care for Mode One Behavior.*

How can you usually identify an Erotic Hypocrite? Similar to WPs, anytime you approach an EH, and express your sexual desires and interests to them in a Mode One manner, they will typically respond with an almost hysterically adverse reaction. *"I beg your pardon??!!" "How dare you talk to me like that!!!" "You don't even KNOW ME!!!" "Do you know what type of guys I date??!!"* These are all common responses from your average EH. Just like a WP, an EH will usually *harshly criticize* your manner of expression, but if they're interested in you, *they will never make an attempt to [immediately] end their interaction with you.* If an EH is attracted to you, and curious about having sex with you, they will *test you* to see if you're going to *apologize* or become *defensive*. **If you do, you are dead meat.** If you stand your ground, and behave composed and unaffected by their opinionated insults and subjective criticisms, they will usually give in to your desires.

Again ... EHs *love sex. The kinkier, the better.* The reason why they publicly pretend not to, is because EHs are very materialistic status seekers. They want to date men who are going to play up to them, spoil them, and generally let them have their way. They know that a Mode One man will *never do that.* An EH is the type of woman who will usually marry a Mode Three "Target" type, but will want to have an affair with a man who exhibits Mode One Behavior (don't do it!).

Why do EHs like to play manipulative head games? They are no different than WPs in this respect: They want to 'have their cake and eat it too.' *(Again ... This is the basic motivation for all WPs and EHs)* In the same manner that most WPs are similar to a man who exhibits Mode Two Behavior, EHs' behavior is very similar to **a man who exhibits Mode Three Behavior.** *Mode Three "Targets" and EHs are almost a perfect match.* An EH will indefinitely hide their true sexual interests from the men they date, and even marry. If they have a 'questionable' sexual history (i.e., past promiscuous behavior, a streak of casual flings, etc), they will do *just about anything* to keep that a secret. EHs will ___never___ attempt to have casual sex with a man who they perceive as a potential husband. **NO WAY.** Usually, the only time they will engage in casual, raunchy, kinky sex is with a man who they know will emphasize discretion and privacy (the men who more than likely, they would never marry). As I mentioned, EHs will usually have the type of sex they *really like* with someone **other than** their boyfriend, fiancé, or husband. Why not with their significant other? **Because this would totally ruin the manipulative game that they are trying to play.**

WHY MEN LOVE PORNO MOVIES and WOMEN LOVE CHICK FLICKS

Most women are under the mistaken impression that the only reason why men love to watch adult films (i.e. "porno flicks") is simply because of the explicit sex scenes. I would beg to differ.

Admittedly, most pornographic adult films made today have no true plot, storylines, or entertaining characters. Most of them, honestly, are **garbage.** But in the 70s and 80s, there were actually some adult films produced that are considered to this day to be "classics."

One of my personal favorites, which relates to the content of this book, is a movie written & directed by Anthony Spinelli entitled "Talk Dirty To Me." This movie stars an adult film actor by the name of John Leslie, who plays the character of "Jack," who is an incorrigible womanizing slacker. His best friend, "Lenny," is just the opposite. A complete loser with women.

Many mainstream publications even ranked this film as one of the Top 20 Best Adult Films of All-Time. What makes this film so entertaining? Trust me ... the actual "sex scenes" in the film are secondary, if not irrelevant. It's the character of "Jack," and how he interacts with women, that is so captivating. "Jack" (John Leslie) is definitely MODE ONE.

Jack literally has **no fear** whatsoever of opinionated insults or subjective criticisms directed at him by women. I mean, absolutely none. He has **no fear** of being rejected by women. I mean, absolutely none. He never attempts to lie to women in order to seduce them, and he never attempts to engage in "manipulative head games" in order to persuade the women into having sex with him. He is just very **bold,** **self-confident,** **upfront** and **unapologetically straightforward**, and he never behaves in an apologetic and/or defensive manner in response to harsh criticisms and insults of his behavior, or his raunchy, provocative manner of verbally expressing his sexual desires, interests, and intentions to women.

Nine times out of ten, you would never see a character like "Jack" in a mainstream film. Why? Because most female movie fans would not want to see that type of character on screen. Why? Because a character like "Jack" **exposes** how duplicitous and manipulative most women are in regards to their own sexual desires. You can argue that, or debate that if you want, but **in my opinion**, it's the truth. Many mainstream movies like for their characters to be either totally "good," or totally "bad." Most male characters are either morally flawless, or they're completely evil. Same with many of the female characters. They are either presented as "innocent, wholesome, prudish good girls," or complete "whores" and/or "bitches." In real life, the vast majority of women fall somewhere in-between those two extremes.

Honest truth? I don't care for most of the male characters in many of the PG, PG-13, and R-rated films that have been produced over the years under the category of "romantic drama" and/or "romantic comedy." There are a few exceptions. I loved Vince Vaughn's character of "Trent" in "Swingers." His character was refreshingly "real." I though Jon Favreau did an excellent job creating his own character of "Mike," to play off of Trent. There are a few other roles I could mention.

Another "realistic" chick flick was "Chasing Amy." I love that movie. This movie goes to the heart of how many men think. Specifically, most men typically can't handle knowing that their girlfriend, or the woman they desire to be their next girlfriend, has engaged in "kinky, promiscuous" sex in their past. Most guys always want their girlfriend, or wife, to have the image and reputation of a "good girl." *Chasing Amy* was probably the best movie I've seen that dealt with this issue.

In most "chick flicks," the behavior of the men is just way too unrealistic for me. For starters, most of the men in most mainstream films are almost totally centered on long-term, monogamous relationships. That's nice to feed into the "fairytale romance" desires of most women, but the harsh fact is, it's **unrealistic**. Most single men I know, especially between the ages of 18 and 29, want casual sex just as much, if not more, than they do [monogamous] relationship sex. I'm just being **real**.

Some women argue that most adult films are "misogynistic," and most of the women in adult films are nothing but "whores." I

ALAN ROGER CURRIE

partially disagree with that. If you watch "Talk Dirty To Me," "Talk Dirty To Me, Part II," or "Nothing To Hide," I believe these adult films portray women fairly **realistically**. There are many women who enjoy episodes of kinky, casual sex just as much as men do. Does that automatically make them a "whore?" I think not.

Most women love "chick flicks" because just about all of those types of movies usually conclude with some couple getting married, or at minimum, finding "true love." Again, that is a great Hollywood business move in order to attract women to the theaters who dream of that "fairy tale romance" scenario, but most "chick flicks" will never hold the interest of most single men.

I will list about eight mainstream "chick flick" films that I did find entertaining (primarily, because the behavior of the male and female characters was **real**), that dealt with being single, dating, and male-female relationships:

- "Swingers" (Jon Favreau, Vince Vaughn)
- "Chasing Amy" (Ben Affleck, Jason Lee)
- "In The Company Of Men" (Aaron Eckhart, Matt Malloy)
- "The Tao Of Steve" (Donal Logue, Greer Goodman)
- "She's Gotta Have It" (Spike Lee, Tracy Camilla Johns)
- "Risky Business" (Tom Cruise, Rebecca De Mornay)
- "Love Jones" (Larenz Tate, Nia Long)
- "Something's Gotta Give" (Jack Nicholson, Diane Keaton)

I'm not suggesting that any movie that has the main male character in pursuit of a long-term, emotionally profound, monogamous relationship is "unrealistic" and/or "sappy," but it's more so about how he goes about pursuing that sort of relationship. Take the movie, "Something's Gotta Give" with Jack Nicholson. He eventually develops a desire for a romantic relationship with Diane Keaton, but his behavior was still **very realistic**. He was very resistant initially, but then he ultimately gives in to his emotional feelings for Keaton's character.

Most men I know don't go out anxiously "looking" for a relationship. Especially, if they're above-average looking, and enjoy a certain degree of popularity with single women. For most men, "serious relationships" usually develop **unexpectedly**. You literally just wake up one day, and realize that you want to spend more and more time with a woman in an exclusive manner. More often than not, that usually happens after you've spent a considerable amount of time in that particular woman's presence.

Other than the "hot sex scenes," and the beautiful bodies of the women, I'm going to tell you why most men love to watch certain adult films more so than traditional "chick flicks":

- You rarely see men having to "flatter women," and/or "wine & dine" women, in order to get them to have sex. Deep-down, most men don't like to feel obligated to use either one of those highly manipulative tactics. Over 90% of the reason why most men excessively flatter women, and/or very quickly offer to 'wine & dine' them, is to motivate them to have sex with them.

- You rarely see women disrespecting men in adult films. In real life, and in many mainstream chick flicks, men are frequently humiliated, rejected, ignored, and/or disrespected by women.

- You rarely see women (or men) exhibiting heavy-duty emotions in adult films. Men don't really care for heavy emotional material in "chick flicks." Men get emotional over come-from-behind Super

Bowl victories, and closely competitive World Series games. Men don't like to get too "emotional" over dating relationships.

- In many "chick flicks," many of the male characters are almost "overly eager" to enter into a serious, long-term, monogamous relationship. In real life, that is not the case for most men. Most men, and particularly, handsome men with above-average popularity, usually have to be "persuaded" to become monogamous with one woman.

Most men don't think about "true love." That is a female thing. When most men initially meet women, the #1 thing on their mind is having sex. Again, it's usually not only until after a man really has spent some quality time interacting with a woman over a period of weeks and/or months that he begins to see her as more than just a satisfying sex partner. Some women may think that is "shallow," or "immature," but that is **real**.

So here's the recap: **Wholesome Pretenders** are those women who want to enjoy the social lifestyle of a woman who gets to enjoy the pleasures of frequent episodes of casual and/or promiscuous sex, but they want to publicly maintain the image and reputation of an innocent, wholesome, sexually conservative, monogamous, and 'marriageable' woman; Therefore, WPs lead a "double life," in which they behave one way in public, and another way in private.

WPs don't particularly care for men who exhibit Mode One Behavior, because such behavior forces them to reveal *who they really are*; Mode

One Behavior forces WPs to either 'pretend' as though they're "offended," "insulted," and "turned off" by provocatively straightforward behavior, **or** it forces them to acknowledge that they share the same exact interests; Either way, they are not able to play the manipulative games they're accustomed to playing with men who exhibit Mode Two and/or Mode Three Behavior.

Erotic Hypocrites are those women who have a specific desire to date and marry men with a high degree of wealth, education, and/or social status. Publicly, they tend to criticize men and other women who engage in kinky or 'unconventional' sexual practices, even though behind closed doors they love raunchy, kinky sex just as much, if not more, than those they criticize; Therefore, EHs also lead a "double life," in which they behave one way towards the men who they're interested in dating and marrying, but a totally different manner towards men who they just want to exchange orgasms with while enjoying one or more episodes of casual sex.

EHs don't particularly care for men who exhibit Mode One Behavior, because such behavior lets them know immediately that *they won't be able to have their way*; Men who exhibit Mode One Behavior would never use their wealth, social connections, or material trappings as a means of gaining a woman's attention and interest. A man exhibiting Mode One Behavior would never "spoil" a woman with gifts and financial favors. Consequently, they are not able to play the manipulative games they're accustomed to playing with men who exhibit Mode Two and/or Mode Three Behavior.

This is why Wholesome Pretenders and Erotic Hypocrites DESPISE the effectiveness of Mode One Behavior. They despise Mode One Behavior because *they know it has the potential to expose them for who they really are, and what they really want.*

What's so bad about both forms of behavior (WP behavior and EH behavior) is that **it is indirectly caused by the judgmental behavior of men.** Women's **fear** of being categorized as a promiscuous "whore," or a kinky "freak" is what usually leads to the duplicitous and manipulative behavior exhibited by Wholesome Pretenders and Erotic Hypocrites.

Men: Quit placing unfair, subjective moral judgments on women. Don't persuade them to have sex with you quickly, and then turn around and bad mouth them to your friends. *All you're doing is motivating women to exhibit more and more **manipulative behavior** towards other men.*

Women: Quit being **deceptive** and **manipulative** for the sake of finding a husband. Marry a man who loves you for *who you really are,* instead of marrying a man who loves you for *who they think you are.* The truth <u>ALWAYS</u> has a way of **revealing itself.**

"Is there anything else I need to be prepared for before you talk about Mode One Behavior?"

Actually, yes. The fear of being criticized, disliked, rejected, and/or ignored is not the only fears that lead to Mode Two and Mode Three Behavior. **There is at least one more fear.** Read on.

CHAPTER SEVEN

The "Other" Fear:
The "Alpha Male Syndrome"
and The Fear Of Being
"Player Hated"

"It's not the fear of failure that prevents most people from reaching their potential for great success; Underachievement is caused just as much by a fear of SUCCESS. Why would anyone fear success? When you're successful, your relationships change. Your friendships change. Some friends and acquaintances will become envious of you. Jealous of you. And this fear of jealousy and envy, if you let it, will prevent you from doing what you have to do to in order to become successful."
Advice from my late father, Clarence Currie, a few years ago

Jealousy and Envy. I've already discussed in detail how the fear of being harshly criticized by a woman will typically lead a man to exhibit Mode Two Behavior. Similarly, a man will exhibit Mode Three Behavior when he's deeply afraid of being rejected and/or ignored by a woman. But there is actually another fear that prevents men from exhibiting the necessary confidence and charm that usually comes along with Mode One Behavior: **THE FEAR OF BEING "PLAYER HATED."**

Ever since the Rap/Hip-Hop generation has made it's presence known in the music industry, there have been certain slang terms that have infiltrated mainstream vernacular. If there is one term that has seemed to stick around indefinitely, it's the term "player hating" *(also known simply as "hating" or "playa hating"). "Don't hate the player, hate the game!"* is frequently expressed by young men and women. **What is a "player hater?"** *Anytime you express a dislike for someone for no other reason than simply the fact that you're jealous and envious of their social status, level of success, and/or popularity with others, you're guilty of "player hating."*

There is nothing that will cause a man to be player hated **by other men** more than when you have a higher degree of romantic and sexual popularity with women than they do. There are many men, plain and simply, THAT HATE THIS. I once read a book where one psychologist actually suggested that one of the primary factors that causes unnecessary male-on-male violence is jealousy and envy towards a man who is more romantically and sexually popular with women than themselves. This phenomenon actually happens in the animal world.

Male animals conduct the whole process of dating far different than intelligent, human males. Their world is much more **VICIOUS** and **COMPETITIVE**. In most animal kingdoms, there is what's known as **THE ALPHA MALE**. The Alpha Male is usually the male who is *the* *most physically dominant* of all the males. He is the male who either has the best fighting and survival skills and/or is the least afraid of killing another male in his kingdom. *Everything about that particular kingdom, particularly in regards to how the males and female mate, trickles down from the Alpha Male.*

In various animal kingdoms, the Alpha Male gets the *first pick* of the high quality females. The second most dominant male gets the second pick, the third most dominant male gets the third pick, and so on and so on. If you're a "submissive" male (i.e., "Beta Male"), you get the "leftovers" (i.e., The low quality females who the more dominant males don't want). If a dominant male sees a submissive male with a female who he wants to mate, he will typically either *boldly take that female away* (sometimes, even during copulation), or *challenge the submissive male to a fight* (usually, to the death). In many ways, there are **human males who** take on these same attitudes.

There are a lot of men who just inherently *don't like* other men who are more handsome than them, make more money than them, have a higher degree of education than them, or are more intelligent and personable than them, if they feel these attributes and characteristics make these men more appealing to women than themselves (see Chapter Four on 'egotistical insecurities'). *They don't necessarily TRY to be this way, they just ARE.* Deep down in their mind, their underlying attitude is *"if you can't outfight me or dominate me physically, there is no way you should be more popular with women than me..."* It's this attitude, that either resides in their conscious mind or subconscious mind, that ends up provoking what's known as "player hater" behavior, and is representative of **THE ALPHA MALE SYNDROME** (AMS).

Well-known comedian Chris Rock had a funny bit about AMS in one of his stand-up performances. He talked about how some guys in the "hood" (i.e., an urban, low-income area) wouldn't really be motivated to earn a college degree, because many of their old peers in the neighborhood would probably say something like, "I don't give a fu** if you have a degree! You're still a punk, and you still can't whup my a**!" Believe it or not, there are many men who actually maintain this unfortunate attitude.

I can name times in both high school and college when I've seen guys literally start a fight with another guy simply because they were jealous and envious of that guy's popularity with women. Typically, if a man perceives you as being more physically dominant or athletic than himself, or a better fighter than himself, he'll usually go ahead and grant you the respect of a ladies' man without a challenge. But if a man thinks that you're a "nerd," a "geek," a "snob," or worse, a "wimp," and you're attracting more attention from women than them, **they will RESENT YOU, and may even try to CHALLENGE YOU.**

And it's this very FEAR of being resented and challenged that causes most men to "suppress" their natural confidence and charm with women. This has actually happened to me on certain occasions. I can name times when I was younger, where I may have attended a party, a nightclub, or a social function, and I actually "held back" on my confidence and personable ways with women I was interacting with, primarily because I didn't want the other men around me to develop any type of jealousy, envy, and/or resentment towards me.

A lot of men don't like to admit it, or sometimes they're not consciously aware that they do this, but they are guilty of it. I've observed many men, who when they're in the company of men who they are close friends with, they will behave more natural and confident in their social interactions with women. But when they are around strange men who they are unfamiliar with, they will suppress their normal sense of self-confidence and charisma. The latter comes from a **FEAR OF BEING PLAYER HATED**.

Don't allow this fear to inhibit your behavior. Unlike animals, most men are not going to challenge you to a no-rules fight for the right to date a woman. Women **choose** on their own what men they want to spend time with. *Don't be a <u>wimp</u> in allowing this fear to dominate your thoughts and behavior while socializing with women.* If other men have a problem with your popularity with other women, that's THEIR PROBLEM ... **NOT YOURS.**

There are actually many men in prison right now because of their "player hating" ways. There are some men who just cannot accept the idea of a man who's not as athletic as them, not as strong as them, not as good a fighter as them, or not as fearless towards killing someone as them, enjoying a better life than them (i.e., a bigger house, a more expensive car, a better job, a higher degree of popularity with women, etc). Deep down, they think JUST LIKE ANIMALS. Again, in certain animal kingdoms, THE MOST FEARLESS, DOMINANT MALES RUN THE SHOW. All of the other males answer to them. They get the first pick of the quality females.

For those men who are guilty of being player haters and possessing AMS characteristics: **WE'RE HUMAN BEINGS, NOT ANIMALS.** Challenge the wrong guy to a fight, and *you might get SHOT.* Animals don't know how to use guns or weapons. So think twice before attempting to "punk" a man who you perceive as being "weak" for the purpose of wanting to steal his woman away.

For those men who are afraid of being player hated: **DON'T CONCERN YOURSELF WITH WHAT OTHER MEN THINK ABOUT YOU AND YOUR POTENTIAL TO BE POPULAR**

WITH WOMEN. Don't let them scare you into exhibiting a lower degree of self-confidence, personal charm, and charisma. *THEIR JEALOUSY AND ENVY IS THEIR PROBLEM* . . . NOT YOURS.

Before you proceed to the eighth and final chapter, answer the following questions:

1) Have you ever 'suppressed' your natural charm, charisma, and self-confidence towards women because you were afraid of another man becoming jealous or envious of you??

2) Have you ever 'player-hated' on another man because you perceived him as being more successful and/or popular with women than you??

After you answer the above two questions, you can finally proceed to **MODE ONE.**

CHAPTER EIGHT

The Men who Exhibit MODE ONE Behavior: The "Self-Assured Straightshooters"

"If you are afraid of being rejected, this fear will affect almost every area of your life – friends, intimate relationships, job interviews, and so on. Rejection is rejection – wherever it is found. So you begin to protect yourself, and, as a result, greatly limit yourself. You begin to shut down and close out the world around you."
Dr. Susan Jeffers, author of <u>Feel the Fear and Do It Anyway</u>

Mode One Behavior. Why is it necessary to exhibit Mode One Behavior? What makes Mode One Behavior so much more effective than Mode Two and Mode Three Behavior? How will my interactions and relationships with women immediately improve as a direct result of expressing myself in a Mode One manner? Questions, questions, questions. Speaking of questions, I have one for you right now:

*How would you approach women, and behave towards women, if you knew for a **100% fact ahead of time** that <u>each</u> and <u>every</u> woman you interacted with was dying to date you, kiss you, and eventually have sex with you, even if they failed to **initially** reveal this to you??*

Don't answer too quickly. Think about this question for a moment. I'm talking about if you knew for a **definite fact** that no matter how a woman initially responded to you, you would eventually be able to get her to enthusiastically reciprocate all of your romantic and sexual desires and interests. Hmmm. Something to think about huh? While you're pondering over this question, let's discuss some important issues regarding your current attitudes and beliefs towards interacting with the opposite sex.

CHANGE SOME OF YOUR EXISTING BELIEFS AND ASSUMPTIONS

The only reason you're reading this book is because, at one time or another in your past, one or more women left you feeling angry, egotistically frustrated, bitter, and/or misogynistic. If you're not willing to admit to yourself that you haven't experienced any of these emotions after interacting with women, then you're wasting your time reading this book. It will not help you, because **you're not allowing it to help you**. This book is a **self-help** book. That means, you have to take it upon **yourself**, to make attempts to **help yourself**.

As I alluded to in my introduction, most books that center on improving your success with women tend to lie about, or mislead you into believing that you can attract any and every woman who you meet and talk to. **NOT TRUE.** The realistic fact of the matter is, there are some women on this earth who are not attracted to you, never have been, and never will be. No matter what you change or improve about your looks, personality, or level of career and financial success, there are a group of women who will **never, ever, ever** find themselves interested in dating you or having sex with you. That's a harsh truth to accept, but a necessary one.

Rejection is not only inevitable in your continuing pursuit of the ideal companion, it is **necessary**. Did you hear me? Are you sure? Let me repeat this again. *Rejection is not only inevitable, but it is necessary.* There is a phrase that says "Rejection is God's protection." You are not meant to hook up with every woman you meet, no matter how attractive, charming, or sexy you may perceive her to be. Not all women are right for you.

Think about if **you** couldn't reject any woman who expressed an interest in dating you, or having sex with you. You know, as well as I do, that there are some women who you would **never** want to date or have sex with, regardless of if they lost weight or gained weight, got a better job, made more money, or changed their religion. When you're just flat out, 100%, genuinely not interested in dating a woman or having sex with a woman, there is very little, if anything, that this woman can do to change your mind. When you "flip the script," you realize that having the power to 'reject' (i.e. not reciprocate someone else's desires and interests) a woman is necessary in order for you to find the women who are <u>right</u> for you, and to allow them to find the men who are <u>right</u> for them.

The quickest and most effective means of diminishing, if not <u>eliminating</u>, your **fear of rejection** is to realize that, in the long-run, **rejection is <u>necessary</u> and <u>beneficial</u>.** When a woman who you're very attracted to declines your invitation to go out on a date, it sometimes can be a hard thing for your ego to accept. But that egotistical disappointment will soon go away. It always does.

The other major fear that affects men's egos is the **fear of harsh, subjective criticism.** Many men want to be 'liked' and have good things said about them constantly. My belief is, anytime *every woman who meets you* has nothing but good, positive things to say about you, that means that nine times out of ten, you're not really being your **true self** with every one of them. When you're truly being yourself, there is **always** going to be at least one characteristic about you that women are going to find undesirable and/or frustrating to their egos.

The biggest thing you need to realize in order to make the **biggest change and improvement you'll ever make in your life** regarding your interactions with women, is to realize that <u>**your**</u> <u>**ego**</u> **is the #1 cause of most of your problems and frustrations with women.**

"What?? Are you calling me egotistical??" **No.** I'm not necessarily calling you 'egotistical,' but I am telling you that your ego is what causes you to experience **anger, frustration,** and **bitterness** anytime you don't receive the responses and reactions that you desire from the women who you're romantically and/or sexually interested in.

I'm going to tell you a big 'secret' to immediately improving your verbal communication skills with women:

You Cannot Allow Your <u>EGO</u> To Become <u>Too</u> <u>Attached</u> To Receiving SPECIFIC Reactions And Responses From Women.

I can pretty much guarantee you … once you remove your ego out of the equation in your interactions with women, your conversational style will become more real, and more objective. A lot of men think that their ego is the source of their self-confidence and sense of ambition. **THIS IS NOT TRUE.** You could, and would, accomplish more in life if you actually **diminish the influence of your ego.** Your level of <u>self-confidence,</u> and your <u>ego,</u> are **not the same thing.** Self-confidence has to do with your desire and ability to **take action** towards the achievement of a desired goal or objective. Your ego centers on **how you perceive yourself,** and **how you believe you're being perceived by others.**

If you attend a social event, and you see an attractive woman, and you **don't hesitate** to <u>take</u> <u>action</u> towards approaching her, that is representative of being **self-confident**, and **self-assured**. When you approach a woman, and converse with a woman, without giving any thought to the "fear" of being criticized and/or rejected, that is representative of being **self-confident**, and **self-assured**.

When you're being self-confident, and self-assured, the only thing on your mind is identifying a desirable goal or objective, and taking whatever action you need to in order to achieve that goal or objective.

It's your ego that causes you to become concerned with other people's perceptions of what you're saying, how you're saying it, and when you're saying it. **Your ego causes you to become obsessed with how people respond to you, and your behavior.** When you're guilty of being too "egotistical," that essentially means that your behavior is heavily influenced by the <u>compliments</u> and <u>criticisms</u> of **other people.** You never want to put yourself in a position where your behavior can be easily manipulated by flattery and/or insults expressed by others.

The **irony** of it is that many times, when you exhibit non-egotistical behavior, many women will label you as 'cocky.' 'Cocky' has a connotation of being 'egotistical.' Many people, including women, tend to think that if you're not driven by the thoughts and opinions of other people, that means that you're 'arrogant' and/or 'cocky.' **THAT IS THE FURTHEST THING FROM THE TRUTH.**

COMPLIMENTS AND CRITICISMS

Two of the most effective psychological tools that people use in order to manipulate others are **compliments** and **criticisms.** More specifically, they use **insincere flattery** and **subjective criticisms.** There is nothing too wrong with expressing **sincere** compliments and **objective** criticisms, as long as it's not an excessive habit, but you need to **train your mind** to ignore and remain <u>unaffected</u> by insincere flattery, subjective criticisms, and/or opinionated insults.

When you become too excited in response to flattery, and too angry or depressed in response to criticism, this is not a good thing. If *manipulative people* detect this characteristic in you, they will **always** try to take advantage of this. This is why you have to strive for <u>egotistical</u> <u>indifference.</u> **This is the #1 basis for the effectiveness of Mode One Behavior.**

Some men spend their entire adult life attempting to prevent and/or avoid a number of subjective criticisms, opinionated insults, and personal 'labels,' such as "immature jerk," "shallow womanizer," or "rude asshole." **These "labels" mean <u>nothing</u>**. People use these criticisms and insults in an attempt to *manipulate you* into exhibiting behavior that is more pleasing, flattering, and accommodating **to them**. Don't allow yourself to fall into the tiresome, misleading trap of trying to avoid critical "labels."

In Order To Consistently Exhibit Mode One Behavior, You Have To Maintain A State Of <u>Egotistical</u> <u>Indifference</u>

DON'T CONCENTRATE ON THE FLAWS AND WEAKNESSES OF WOMEN

Mode Two Behavior and Mode Three Behavior ALWAYS eventually lead to Mode Four Behavior. Mode Two Behavior is *effective,* but *weak.* Mode Three Behavior is *weak **AND** ineffective.*

As I've alluded to before, the problem is **not** with the woman's behavior. You might fool yourself into believing that it is, but in reality, it's not. Deep, deep down, you're really angry, frustrated, and bitter at **YOURSELF**. Once again, "weak" behavior is any behavior that you exhibit that opens the door for women to manipulate you, take advantage of you, disrespect you, and/or generally treat you in an undesirable manner. **Weak behavior** is any behavior that is *too lenient, too respectful, too accommodating,* and/or *too flattering.*

What most men don't realize, is that when you constantly criticize women (e.g., "all women are bitches!!"), you're basically saying to your subconscious mind that **"women have power over me and my emotions."** When it comes to changes and improvements in behavior, **only concentrate on your own behavior.** Don't concern yourself with the flaws and weaknesses you perceive women as having. Why? For one thing, **you have absolutely no control over women's behavior.** Only women have the power to improve the flaws and weaknesses in their behavior. You only have control over **how you behave towards women**, and **how you allow them to behave towards you.**

Don't Concern Yourself With What You 'Like' or 'Dislike' About Women's Behavior; Only Concentrate On Your OWN Behavior

WEAK VS. INEFFECTIVE BEHAVIOR

In general, weak AND ineffective behavior will hurt your chances of maintaining a woman's romantic and sexual interest. But honestly, if I had to choose between the two, **weak** behavior is much more detrimental to your emotions, and sense of self-confidence, than **ineffective** behavior. **Ineffective** behavior (i.e., behavior that is counterproductive to the achievement of your desired goals and objectives in a relationship) is primarily the result of waiting too long to express what's really on your mind to a woman. You're hesitating too long before revealing your true needs, desires, interests, and intentions. For the most part, that's an easy fix.

Weak behavior is more challenging to correct. Weak behavior, as mentioned before, is predicated on some deep, profound **fears** that you possess, and to some degree, **egotistical insecurities** and **low self-esteem**. In a nutshell, *you don't value your own attention and companionship* as much as the attention and companionship of the women you're pursuing. This is worth repeating:

ANYTIME YOU PLACE MORE VALUE AND SIGNIFICANCE ON THE ATTENTION and COMPANIONSHIP OF A WOMAN, THAN YOU DO YOUR OWN, YOUR BEHAVIOR IS GOING TO BE <u>WEAK</u>.

This is one of the major weaknesses that causes men to exhibit both Mode Two Behavior as well as Mode Three Behavior. Anytime you perceive a woman's attention and companionship as being more worthwhile to you, than yours is to her, you're going to eventually exhibit behavior that is weak. That's not an opinion, that's a hard, cold fact. This leads me to another major principle of Mode One Behavior:

NO WOMAN'S TIME, ATTENTION, OR COMPANIONSHIP IS MORE VALUABLE THAN YOUR OWN.

If it takes repeating this a thousand times to yourself in order to absorb it and believe it, do it. No other principle associated with Mode One Behavior is more important than this one. You can't ever treat a woman's time, attention, and/or companionship as if it is more valuable and significant to you, than yours is to her. If you do, I can pretty much guarantee you that at some point in the future, that woman is going to either get bored with you and lose interest in you, engage in manipulative 'head games' with you, or treat you like a *punk* who she can egotistically 'bully' around when she wants to.

Next to your ego, this is the most significant cause of weak and ineffective behavior towards women. If there is one hard lesson that I've had to painfully learn over and over and over again, it would be that you can **never** excessively flatter women, fawn over women, and/or consistently play up to their egos, and then expect to have long-term success with them. I have **never** met a guy in my entire life who was highly popular with women, and consistently enjoyed successful and satisfying relationships with women, that consistently fawned over women and spoiled them egotistically. Don't fool yourself.

Similar to playing up to a woman's ego, another form of weak behavior you can exhibit is to repeatedly criticize a woman, particularly in a harsh, subjective manner, but turn around and continue to pursue that woman's attention, interest, and companionship. I can guarantee you that women will begin to look at you as a weak-willed wimp. It's okay to criticize women occasionally in an <u>objective</u> manner, but I try my best to avoid expressing harsh, subjective, opinionated criticisms. For many women, criticizing them is like an indirect form of flattery. Because for many women, and manipulative women in particular, when you criticize them, you're acknowledging that they're able to frustrate you, and get under your skin.

What's the best way to let a woman know that you disapprove of her behavior? **Leave her alone.** Ignore her indefinitely until she apologizes for her undesirable behavior towards you, and/or she changes those characteristics that you don't like. **Actions always speak louder than words.** The best way to criticize a woman is with your **actions**. Demonstrate to her that her undesirable behavior has consequences. For me personally, I try not to concern myself with what I 'like' or 'don't like' about a woman's behavior. I only concern myself with what I can **tolerate** over a period of time, and what I can't tolerate over a period of time. Once a woman exhibits behavior that I don't feel as though I can tolerate indefinitely, I'm history. Ciao. Later. I'm on to the next woman of interest.

The best rule of thumb to remember regarding subjective vs. objective criticisms is this: **Never criticize a woman for exhibiting behavior that she never agreed <u>not</u> to exhibit.** If you do, you're guilty of expressing a subjective criticism based on what you personally don't like. **So what.** On the other hand, if a woman is exhibiting behavior that she previously agreed or promised not to exhibit, then it's okay to **objectively criticize** her. But even with objective criticisms, they shouldn't be repeatedly and persistently expressed. After a while, it's time to just move on to the next woman.

<u>Remember</u>: There is a **huge difference** between **desiring** a woman's attention and companionship, and **<u>needing</u>** a woman's attention and companionship. The latter is the root of many aspects of men's weak, and ineffective behavior towards women. When you present yourself as being "needy" of a woman's attention and companionship, it makes you look very **weak** in the eyes of most, if not all women.

NEVER PUT WOMEN ON <u>PEDESTALS</u>

Speaking of moving on to the next woman, this brings me to the fourth primary principle that leads to weak and/or ineffective behavior: expressing an interest in having an exclusive, monogamous relationship with a woman **too quickly.** Don't be so quick to cut off all of your other potential female companions, assuming you have other options. One of the biggest mistakes that I've made with women repeatedly, particularly those who I was interested in romantically, was being 'too anxious' to make my relationship with them an exclusive one. **MISTAKE**.

Within the first few days or weeks after meeting a woman, always treat a woman like she is just **one of many**. I don't care how beautiful a woman is, how sexy a woman is, how intelligent a woman is, or how wholesome and virginal she is. Exclusivity is something I feel as though a woman should have to **earn**. I've had some of my female acquaintances consider that 'shallow' on my part to maintain that attitude. That's not 'shallow' at all. That's **REALITY**. The primary time I've had women express a high interest in me, only to see that interest diminish in less than a month later, has been times when I behaved as though I was too **eager** to be 'exclusive' with that woman. In my experience, I have found that women tend to perceive an overanxious attitude towards exclusivity as a sign of loneliness and desperation. Both are big turn-offs for most women.

When you're in a Mode One state of mind, always talk to women and treat women you've just met as if they are just **one of many** women who you're considering dating or having sex with. The vast majority of women who have pursued my attention and companionship the most aggressively have typically been those who felt like they were in 'competition' with other women for my interest. This is one of the reasons why many women go crazy over male celebrity types. One of the biggest characteristics that enhances many women's interest in a man who is famous is that they know these men have **other women** pursuing them. Even my own mother said once that, *"no woman wants a man who they think no other woman wants."* One of my high school buddies put it best back in the late 80s; he said *"the more popular you already are with women, the more popular you will become with women."* In my experience, I have found this to be very true.

You ever wonder why some men are frequently criticized, but yet still highly pursued by women, while other men are frequently complimented by women, but are very rarely pursued? It's primarily because of the **'one of many' factor**. Most women with **healthy egos** don't like to be treated as though they're just 'one of many' women who you're interested in. So egotistically, this frustrates them. On the other hand though, these same women find these guys more intriguing and appealing because of the fact that they know these guys are **being pursued by other women**.

When you are too quick to treat a woman like she's "the one," you might end up receiving a lot of flattering compliments from that woman, but more than likely, she's going to lose interest in you romantically and sexually. Just about every single time that I've treated a woman as if I was too anxious or eager to date them, or treated them as if they were the only women on earth that I found physically and sexually appealing, those women eventually lost interest in me. I remember one time in 1990, I met this woman, and we chatted on the phone. During the conversation, she said "I bet you are *so popular* with women…" Me, trying to play the Mode Two 'modest' role, replied, "oh, not really. I actually don't have any women pursuing me at the moment. You're pretty much the only one interested in me right now." **I never heard from that female again in life**.

NEVER PUT A WOMAN ON A 'PEDESTAL'; ALWAYS TREAT WOMEN YOU'VE JUST MET AS IF THEY ARE JUST 'ONE OF MANY' WOMEN WHO YOU'RE CURRENTLY INTERESTED IN.

TOO MUCH SMALL TALK

Another major factor that usually leads to weak and ineffective behavior is something I emphasized in Chapter Three, when I discussed Mode Two Behavior: **Talking too much**. When you engage in too much trivial, irrelevant *small talk*, over a period of time, women will begin to look at you as more of a platonic friend more so than a potential romantic companion or lover. Trust me … I've experienced this too many times. Just about every woman who at some point in time told me "Alan, let's just be friends…," it was usually those women who I did a whole lot of **unnecessary "chit-chatting"** with. On the flip side, most of the women who have usually maintained the highest romantic and sexual interest in me were usually those who almost had to beg me to talk to them more than ten to fifteen minutes at a time.

Truthfully, I believe this comes from not having enough activity in your life. More than likely, you're a **time-waster**. You have **too much free time** on your hands. If there is one thing I've noticed about men who live very active, busy lifestyles, is that they don't have time for trivial small talk. For these types of men, **avoiding small talk is not so much a choice as much as it is a necessity**. Most men who are confident and busy are *naturally* Mode One. It's the only way that they can be productive. So anytime you find yourself engaging in an extraordinary amount of small talk with women, you have to ask yourself, "Am I utilizing my time in a wise and productive manner?" More than likely, the answer will be "no."

AS MUCH AS POSSIBLE, ALWAYS AVOID 'SMALL TALK'; SMALL TALK USUALLY LEADS TO PLATONIC FRIENDSHIPS RATHER THAN ROMANTIC or SEXUAL RELATIONSHIPS

ACCOMPLISHMENTS AND MATERIAL POSSESSIONS

The final factor that leads to weak and ineffective behavior is allowing your sense of confidence and self-esteem to be based on external, extrinsic factors such as wealth, material possessions, or career and educational achievements. When you allow 'outer' factors to dictate how good you feel about yourself, you set yourself up for erratic, highly inconsistent levels of self-confidence. Your self-confidence and self-esteem should be based on **inner, intrinsic factors**. Things such as your moral character, your principles and values, and your day-to-day ability to **take action** towards the achievement of your desired goals and objectives. Factors that you have **total control over**, and that cannot be destroyed, diminished, or taken away from you by others.

This is why I don't really believe in 'wining and dining' a woman right off the bat. When you do this too early and/or too frequently, women will begin to take your attention and companionship for granted. They will not develop a **genuine** interest in your company, but rather they will begin to look at you as just a means of obtaining a free lunch, a free dinner, or a free movie or concert. In my personal experience, the women who I spent the most money on in the first three to four weeks after meeting them were the women who I very rarely, if ever, ended up dating or having sex with. Most of the women who I have dated or had sex with, I spent very little money on them within the first one or two months after I met them. It wasn't until I knew them for a while that they began to get "treated."

MODE ONE

WHY MODE ONE BEHAVIOR REPLACES MODE TWO BEHAVIOR

As mentioned before, the problem with Mode Two behavior is that it is too cautious, too indirect, and too slow. In addition, it's too lenient and too accommodating. When you exhibit Mode Two Behavior, you're taking a 'gamble' of sorts; You're basically saying to a woman subconsciously, "If I behave in a manner that is pleasing, flattering, and accommodating to your ego, I'm betting that you will demonstrate your gratitude by reciprocating my romantic and sexual interests." When you exhibit Mode Two Behavior, you tend to put too much emphasis on being perceived as a "gentleman," and having a woman "like" you, and say good things about you to their other female friends. *It's these objectives that ultimately weaken the effectiveness of your verbal communication style.* In reality, women don't date you, or choose to have sex with you, because you're 'nice' to them, say all the 'right things,' and/or leave a 'favorable impression' on them. **Just because a woman 'likes' you, and thinks highly of your personality and behavior, does not necessarily mean that she wants to date you, or sexually aroused by you.**

Women develop a desire to spend time with you in a romantic and/or sexual manner because something about you *turns them on.* Something about the way you look, and the manner in which you behave, *arouses them.* Among other things, a high degree of **self-confidence** and **self-assurance** is a known psychological aphrodisiac.

I've read numerous articles in which women have frequently said that the #1 non-physical turn-on in a man is their level of self-confidence and self-assurance. This is why Mode One Behavior is generally *more appealing* to women than Mode Two Behavior. Mode One Behavior causes you to *naturally* come across as more self-confident, more self-assured, and more provocative. **For one thing, you have to be self-confident simply to exhibit Mode One Behavior.** Mode One Behavior is not for the verbally wimpy types.

Honestly, it has been my experience that playing the "Mr. Nice Guy / Mr. Perfect Gentleman" role may work for you in the **short run**, but in the long run, most women are generally going to want nothing more from you than a good, entertaining **platonic** relationship with you. Trust me … *I've experienced this too many times*, and probably no less than 90% of the men I know have told me that they've experienced the same thing. Very rarely have I developed a long-lasting romantic or sexual relationship with a woman as a direct result of exhibiting Mode Two Behavior. One reason, is because deep down, *women know that you're attempting to play up to their ego.* They know that you're exhibiting "gentlemanly" behavior for the sake of *pleasing them.* Consequently, they know deep down that if *they really wanted to*, they could *manipulate you*, and *have their way with you.* And for most women, **that is not a challenge to their ego.** Generally speaking, women are not sexually aroused by men who they know they can easily manipulate and/or egotistically dominate.

Mode One Behavior is a more demanding, and non-manipulative version of Mode Two Behavior. Mode Two Behavior is much better than Mode Three Behavior, but it isn't quite as effective as Mode One Behavior. Mode One Behavior doesn't have the intention of manipulating women, nor does it allow or invite manipulative behavior. **Just straight up, honest, unapologetic truth**. If a woman can't handle hearing what your true, honest desires, interests, and intentions are, **that's HER PROBLEM. NOT YOURS.**

If your only interest in approaching a woman is to have one weekend of kinky, casual sex ... why 'beat-around-the-bush'?? What can she do ... REJECT YOU?? **So what.** **Again, rejection from women is inevitable and necessary.** What if she CRITICIZES YOU for having shallow, immoral objectives?? **So what.** Who is she to judge you. What if she thinks that your manner of expression is TOO FORWARD?? **So what.** Time is valuable. You don't have time to waste. And besides ... that's *her* opinion. **Always ignore subjective criticisms and opinionated insults.** Unless you're a man who is guided solely by his ego, those criticisms and insults mean **nothing**.

MODE ONE BABY ... MAKE IT HAPPEN.

WHY MODE ONE BEHAVIOR ELIMINATES MODE THREE BEHAVIOR

Mode One Behavior is the direct *antithesis* of Mode Three Behavior. They have absolutely NO similarities. **Mode Three behavior is a totally <u>fear-based</u> form of behavior. Mode One Behavior is a <u>principle-based</u> and <u>confidence-based</u> form of behavior.** Mode Three is phony and pretentious; Mode One Behavior is all the way **real.** Mode Three Behavior is misleading, deceptive, and timid; Mode One Behavior is **open, honest,** and **boldly straightforward.** There's really only one reason why men feel compelled to lie to women, mislead women, and manipulate women into giving them the attention and interest they want: **They're cowards.** They are **verbal wimps.** They want something from women (attention, interest, companionship, etc), but they're afraid to confidently and directly ask for it. **A man who exhibits Mode Three Behavior is totally paralyzed by a fear of either being rejected or ignored by women.**

If you're a Mode Three "Timid," then you need to simply develop some **courage.** In the movie "Three Kings," Cpl. Archie Gates (George Clooney) says to Soldier Conrad Vig (Spike Jonze), "You're scared, right? The way it works is, you do the thing you're **scared sh**less of,** and **you get the courage AFTER you do it,** <u>not</u> **before** you do it." That pretty much sums up **Mode One** Behavior: Confidence and courage is not representative of NOT HAVING ANY FEAR(S), but rather, it's **<u>TAKING ACTION DESPITE HAVING FEARS</u>.** The more you consistently *take action* (e.g., approach women in a confident manner, express your desires straightforwardly and upfront, etc.), the more you will see that your 'fears' will begin to diminish. Fear of rejection is nothing more than the result of allowing your **ego** to become 'too attached' to the idea of receiving a specific response or reaction from women. **Your ego can be your friend and YOUR ENEMY.**

If you're a Mode Three "Target," you *pretend* as though you have confidence towards women, but your sense of confidence is *phony*. You base your confidence on material possessions and extrinsic achievements. Your false confidence comes from things like how much money you earn, what type of car you drive, what type of neighborhood you live in, or the high status of the job you have. 90% or more of your conversations with women usually revolves around one or more of these superficial characteristics.

On the positive end, *you will attract some women*. You may even attract *beautiful, sexy women*. On the downside though, very few of these women will be **genuinely interested in YOU**. They will want to spend time with you, and share your company so they can take advantage of **what you have**, take advantage of the **material gifts** and **financial favors** you offer, and take advantage of the **high society parties you invite them to**, and the **social connections** you have to offer them. *You are a **magnet** for women who are Erotic Hypocrites and gold diggers.* If you date one of these women, or marry them, I can almost guarantee you that some smooth-talking guy with less money than you, but a **more legitimate sense of self-confidence**, will eventually be exchanging orgasms with your girlfriend or wife. I've seen it happen too many times.

If you have problems getting out of a Mode Three rut, the biggest thing you need to do is begin concentrating on exhibiting behavior that is more SELF-CONFIDENT and STRAIGHTFORWARD. *Don't concern yourself with women's behavior TOWARDS YOU;* Only concern yourself with *your behavior TOWARDS WOMEN.* Don't even think about, or anticipate, whether or not you're going to receive a "positive" or "negative" response from women. Concentrate only on expressing your true needs, desires, interests, and intentions. **Let the response take care of itself.**

Don't allow women to frighten you ("Timids") or use you like a dependable "Sugar Daddy" ("Targets"). No matter what your level of wealth or social status is, **be MODE ONE.** Why hide your true interests from a woman?? What can she do … REJECT YOU?? **So what. Remember:** Rejection prevents you from **wasting time** with women who are not genuinely interested in you. What can she do … IGNORE YOU?? **So what.** That just means she's not your type.

Rejection is <u>necessary</u> for you to move closer to finding your <u>ideal</u> <u>companion</u>.

MODE ONE BABY ... MAKE IT HAPPEN.

WHY MODE ONE BEHAVIOR <u>PREVENTS</u> MODE FOUR BEHAVIOR

The ONLY reason why any man exhibits Mode Four Behavior, is because he previously exhibited Mode Two and/or Mode Three Behavior, and he ended up having his time wasted, his money wasted, and his ego disrespected and crushed. When you exhibit Mode Four Behavior, *you tend to blame everyone else* for your **anger, frustration,** and **bitterness** more than the person who really deserves the blame: **YOU.** Nobody told you to take forever to let women know why you really wanted to share their company! Nobody told you to flatter women every single time you shared their company! Nobody told you to criticize women repeatedly, but then continue to make efforts to spend time with them! Nobody told you to wine and dine women, and immediately treat them like they were "the one." That is **your fault.**

As I mentioned in Chapter Five, Mode Four Behavior is essentially **after-the-fact** Mode One Behavior. Once you've already been criticized, disrespected, manipulated, rejected, and/or ignored ... THEN you all of the sudden begin to express all sorts of harsh criticisms and opinionated insults in a bold and straightforward manner. "The only reason why I talked to you for an hour is because I wanted to have kinky sex with you!!!" Ooooh. Now you're the Big Man. Speaking your mind in an unapologetic manner. **Wake up call:** IT DOESN'T MAKE A DIFFERENCE NOW. Women **don't want to hear** what you have to say, **nor do they expect to hear** what you're expressing. The person you're really angry at, deep down, is **YOURSELF.**

You're really ticked off because you know that you didn't really behave in the manner that you really wanted to behave from the beginning of your interaction. *Deep down, you wanted to express yourself in a boldly confident, unapologetically straightforward, MODE ONE manner, but you wimped out.* Nobody forced you to play the "Mr. Perfect Gentleman" role (well, okay … maybe your domineering mother did). You exhibited Mode Two Behavior … and what did you get? Not even a kiss. Just another platonic female friend.

Nobody forced you to lie to women, avoid women, and/or try to impress women with materialistic possessions and superficial achievements. That was **YOUR CHOICE.** *Your fears and insecurities got the best of you.* And you got **PLAYED.** You got manipulated **BIG TIME.** How much money did those gold diggers charge on your credit card?? How many rent payments did you pay out?? How many expensive dinners did you buy?? Wow. Where are these women who were supposedly "really, really interested in you" now?? You didn't REALLY think they would hang around with you indefinitely did you?? ***There's always another Mode Three "Target" with MORE MONEY and MORE SOCIAL STATUS than you!!*** The EHs and gold diggers go towards the highest bidder. You exhibited Mode Three Behavior … and what did you get? More debt and no long-term companions. **Ouch.**

Someone once said, *"the only way a monkey can ride your back is if it's bent."* I hate to tell you this, but when you frequently exhibit Mode Two Behavior and/or Mode Three Behavior … **your back is BENT.** In a nutshell, the only way that a woman can treat you in an undesirable, disrespectful manner is if you're exhibiting behavior that **ALLOWS THEM TO** treat you in an undesirable, disrespectful manner. That's the **weakness** of both Mode Two and Mode Three Behavior: Those forms of behavior allow women to manipulate you, and generally treat you in an undesirable manner. Why? **Because both forms of behavior are FEAR-BASED BEHAVIOR.** The ONLY reason you exhibit Mode Two Behavior (as opposed to Mode One Behavior) is because you're **AFRAID** of being harshly criticized or disliked. You want every female you meet to think highly of you, and say "good, positive things" about you. ***YOUR FEAR OF WOMEN'S NEGATIVE PERCEPTIONS OF YOU IS DICTATING YOUR BEHAVIOR.***

To exhibit Mode Three Behavior is **even WORSE**. The ONLY reason you exhibit Mode Three Behavior is because you're dreadfully AFRAID of being rejected and/or ignored by a woman. You want some type of attention from women ... even if it's **undesirable** or **disrespectful**. You'd rather be treated like crap, or allow yourself to be 'used,' than to be completely and indefinitely ignored. *YOUR FEAR OF BEING "BLOWN OFF" AND IGNORED BY WOMEN IS DICTATING YOUR BEHAVIOR.*

Now, that you're in a Mode Four state of mind, you try to charm unsuspecting women so that you can eventually bruise their egos and/or cause them emotional turmoil. If you're really out of control, you'll become a rapist or serial killer of women (think Ted Bundy). **You have SO MUCH pent-up anger and frustration from being dumped on by women, that you are bursting at the seams for egotistical revenge.**

How do I transform my Mode Four anger into Mode One excitement? **LET GO OF THE PAST.** *Take the blame for most, if not all, of your failed interactions with women.* Those women in your past took advantage of you because you made it SO EASY for them to do so! Do you engage in a high degree of "trivial small talk?" **QUIT DOING THAT.** Do you go out of your way to flatter women's egos constantly? **QUIT DOING THAT.** Do you frequently offer to spend ridiculous amounts of money on women, and wine & dine women, before you even know if they have a definite interest in dating you? **QUIT DOING THAT!!!**

"Start over," only this time, **be MODE ONE**. Express your real desires, interests, and intentions in the **most CONFIDENT** and **STRAIGHTFORWARD** manner as possible. "What if they criticize me for being too forward?" **SO!!** "What if they don't like my approach?" **SO!!!** "What if they don't reciprocate my desires and interests?" **SO!!!!** "What if they choose to ignore me altogether??" **SO!!!!!** *Are you going to let a handful of not-so-desirable reactions from women prevent you from being who you really want to be???* For the sake of all MANHOOD ... don't let that happen! **Be YOURSELF.** More importantly, **be your CONFIDENT SELF.** YOU are the only person who can prevent you from behaving in a SELF-ASSURED MANNER. **Remember that.**

MODE ONE BABY ... MAKE IT HAPPEN.

THE SEVEN KEY PRINCIPLES TO EXHIBITING MODE ONE BEHAVIOR

Similar to Steven R. Covey's *The Seven Habits of Highly Effective People©*, you can think of the following Mode One principles as the 'seven habits of improving your verbal communication skills with women.' I have found that, generally speaking, when you 'violate' one or more of these seven principles on a regular or semi-regular basis in your interactions with women, you will find yourself typically exhibiting Mode Two Behavior and/or Mode Three Behavior, and consequently, feeling 'angry,' 'egotistically frustrated,' and 'bitter' towards those women who did not reciprocate the interests you had in them (Mode Four Behavior).

Here are the Seven Primary Principles of maintaining a "Mode One" attitude & demeanor:

1) Never hesitate to approach a woman you find attractive. There are only two valid reasons to avoid approaching a woman: a) You're not interested in dating that woman, or having sex with her; b) You're attracted to her, but you already have knowledge that she is married, engaged, or has a serious boyfriend. Other than that, you should never hesitate to approach a woman you're attracted to.

You have to force yourself to **take action**. Consistently **taking action** is what leads to a higher degree of self-confidence, not lack of rejection. I don't care if you approach ten women, and nine of them reject you, just the fact that you took action to approach them is going to improve and increase your sense of self-confidence.

When you first meet a woman who you're interested in, *don't concern yourself with how she's going to respond to you*; Only concern yourself with what your **honest desires, interests, and intentions are**, and concentrate on *expressing them* in *the most self-assured* and *unapologetically straightforward manner as possible.*

2) As much as possible, *always AVOID trivial, inconsequential 'small talk' and/or entertaining, but non-purposeful conversation;* When conversing with a woman, there should <u>ALWAYS</u> be a *specific purpose* for talking with her. You should always be looking to express some sort of specific desire, specific interest, and/or specific intention.

3) Never allow yourself to give a woman too much attention that is exceptionally 'flattering to her ego'; *Always avoid <u>fawning</u> over a woman, or filling her head with <u>excessive</u> <u>compliments;</u>* This shows weaknesses and insecurities in your ego. With the possible exception of if a woman is your wife, fiancée, or your serious girlfriend, you should never flatter a woman's ego too frequently.

4) Always avoid giving a woman the impression that she is the <u>only</u> female who is interested in you romantically and/or sexually; Generally, women lose interest in you if they feel that they are the only ones who are interested in you. *Interest from women attracts interest from other women.* Women are most attracted to men who they know other women find appealing. If you have two or more women interested in you, **don't try to hide that.** If anything, **emphasize it.** Women tend to become more intrigued by you when they perceive themselves as being in 'competition' with other women for your attention, interest, and companionship.

5) Anytime you express a specific desire to share a woman's company, and she asks you something along the lines of "Why should I get together with you?" or "What are we going to do when we hook up?," **DON'T "WIMP OUT."** Let her know in a very confident, self-assured manner what your **SPECIFIC desires, interests, and intentions are;** If she has an adverse reaction to your suggestions (however provocative they may be), *do **NOT** become apologetic and/or defensive;* Always maintain a composure of **cool, calm, confidence.** Wholesome Pretenders and Erotic Hypocrites will almost always criticize you to 'test' you. Most non-manipulative women, if they're not interested, will simply say "I'm not interested" and end their interaction/conversation with you. If a woman doesn't share your same interests, move on to the next female.

6) Never go out of your way to "wine & dine" a woman too quickly, or offer her a variety of monetary and/or materialistic gifts when you're just starting to get to know her; This makes you look like you're **egotistically weak,** and **desperate** for female companionship. A woman should have to **earn the privilege** of having material gifts showered on her by proving her loyalty to you, as well as convincing you that she possesses a true, **genuine interest** in sharing your company romantically and/or sexually.

7) Never criticize, or try to diminish the appeal, of another man's appeal to women; That shows signs of **egotistical insecurity** and **Player Hating** (e.g., *"Oh, that guy is not THAT handsome. . ."* or *"I don't see what women see in that guy"*); Many times, your jealous and envious comments towards that guy will make him seem *more appealing* to the women you're conversing with. In a similar manner, never "whine" and "complain" about what you "don't like" about women's behavior, or express frustration regarding the behavior of ex-girlfriends, ex-lovers, or other women in general. **No woman wants to date a man, or have sex with a man, who they feel is a weak "whiner" type; If you cannot tolerate any aspect of a woman's behavior, simply leave her alone and move on to the next female.**

There you have it. These are the seven primary key principles to remember in order to best maintain a Mode One attitude and demeanor. You can **add some of your own principles** to mine, but the key thing is to **STICK TO THEM**. Don't violate them.

"Will these principles help me attract each and every woman I meet?"

<u>NO</u>. No book written will help you achieve that unrealistically ambitious objective. Not only will you not attract every woman you meet, you shouldn't even **want to** attract every woman you meet. Not every woman you meet is good for you to connect with.

"Will these principles prevent me from being criticized or disliked?"

<u>NO</u>. In many ways, you're probably going to get criticized MORE for being so boldly straightforward with women. If Mode One was **EASY**, *all men would exhibit Mode One Behavior.* <u>Remember</u>: **Wholesome Pretenders** and **Erotic Hypocrites** will <u>always criticize</u> the use of Mode One Behavior ... at least, **initially** (then, they will often times give in to your desires once they see you're not going to *wimp out* and *apologize*).

There is a difference between a woman <u>not</u> being interested in you, and a woman **pretending** not to be interested in you. The first thing you learn in sales is that there is a difference between *rejection* and *resistance.* There are many women who are attracted to you, but they will **resist** the idea of dating you or having sex with you until you give them a **valid, provocative** reason to act on their interest in you.

"Will these principles prevent me from feeling angry, frustrated, or bitter towards women as a result of them rejecting me or manipulating me?"

YES. This is what MODE ONE IS ALL ABOUT. Mode One Behavior will ALWAYS prevent women who are not genuinely interested in you from wasting your time and/or money. What is the 'magical' secret of Mode One Behavior?? It's simply this: *Anytime you express your romantic and/or sexual desires, interests, and intentions to a woman in an extremely honest, self-assured, highly specific, and unapologetically straightforward manner, you virtually FORCE THEM to do the EXACT SAME THING.* Very few, if any women will be able to *lead you on.*

WHEN YOU EXHIBIT TOTALLY NON-MANIPULATIVE BEHAVIOR TOWARDS WOMEN, YOU BASICALLY FORCE THEM TO EXHIBIT TOTALLY NON-MANIPULATIVE BEHAVIOR TOWARDS YOU. This is the key factor that makes Mode One Behavior so effective.

NO MORE MODE TWO BEHAVIOR! Why waste time?

NO MORE MODE THREE BEHAVIOR! Why be afraid?

NO MORE MODE FOUR BEHAVIOR! Why be angry?

As I asked you at the beginning of the chapter … "How would you approach women, and behave towards women, if you knew for a **100% fact** *ahead of time* that <u>each</u> and <u>every</u> woman you interacted with was dying to date you, kiss you, and eventually have sex with you, even if they didn't initially reveal this to you??"

You would APPROACH WOMEN MORE **CONFIDENTLY**.

You would EXPRESS YOURSELF **STRAIGHTFORWARDLY**.

You would BE **TOTALLY UPFRONT** WITH YOUR INTENTIONS

You would **NEVER ANTICIPATE REJECTION**.

You would **IGNORE SUBJECTIVE CRITICISMS**.

You would EXHIBIT MODE ONE BEHAVIOR.

Don't HESITATE.

<u>TAKE</u> <u>ACTION</u>.

BUILD UP YOUR SELF-CONFIDENCE.

Mode One Baby … Make it happen!!

Was this your first time reading this book??

READ IT AGAIN.

READ THIS BOOK OVER, and OVER, and OVER, and OVER AGAIN UNTIL MODE ONE BEHAVIOR BECOMES <u>NATURAL</u> TO YOU.

I SINCERELY THANK YOU FOR PURCHASING THIS BOOK. YOU WON'T REGRET IT.

FREQUENTLY ASKED QUESTIONS

Ever since I developed the concept of the Four Modes Of Verbal Communication™, and began the process of turning this concept into a published book, I've had a number of males, and even females, frequently ask me questions about the Mode One Principles and Philosophy. Here, I will try to answer many of the questions that I've been asked the most frequently:

• *Isn't "Mode One: Let The Women Know What You're REALLY Thinking" just another attempt at another "How To Pick Up Women & Seduce Them" styled book??*

For the most part, I would have to say NO. It is true, that there have been many men who have incorporated the principles of a Mode One attitude and demeanor for the specific purpose of seducing women, but I can't say that this is **my** sole, specific purpose for writing Mode One. For me, I think of being able to attract and seduce women more so as a *fringe benefit* of exhibiting Mode One Behavior, rather than it's specific purpose. If anything, I think the primary purpose of Mode One Behavior is to prevent women from manipulating you and disrespecting you, as well as provide men with a framework for *conquering their fears* of being criticized, disliked, rejected, and/or ignored.

Most men can relate to the idea of the "classroom bully." What do most 'bullies' attempt to do? They try to *intimidate you* and *control you* by *taking advantage of the fears they know you have.* With the 'neighborhood bully,' they take advantage of your fear of being beat up; With the 'mean boss,' it's your fear of being fired that they take advantage of; With 'crooked' cops, it's the fear of being thrown in jail for no reason that they take advantage of. Well, believe it or not, there are attractive, sexy WOMEN who will try to "punk" you (i.e., try to intimidate you and/or control you) too. In the same way a physical bully uses his size or fighting skills, and a mean-spirited supervisor uses their power and job status, many manipulative women use their beauty, their sex appeal, and popularity with other men to "egotistically punk" you.

146

They KNOW that you have a "fear" of being criticized by them, disliked by them, rejected by them, and/or ignored by them, and they take FULL ADVANTAGE OF THIS.

This is what leaves you feeling "angry," "frustrated," and/or "bitter" many times after conversing with a female, after going out on a date with a female, or just generally having a 'bad interaction' with her period. Many times, a man will say that he's "pissed off" because the woman he just talked to, or went out with, was a "total bitch." Deep down though, it's not the woman's behavior that's really bothering him. It's the fact that he *allowed* that female to EGOTISTICALLY PUNK HIM that has him pissed off. How are we, as men, "egotistically punked" by women?

- When a woman's beauty is so stunning, that you fail to even approach them; Why? Because in your mind, you say "I'm afraid of being rejected, or 'blown off' by her"; *She has you afraid to take action!! You just got egotistically punked.*

- When a woman wears sexy, provocative clothes around you, and as a result, you're constantly "fawning" over her, flattering her, and generally playing up to her ego; Why? Because in your mind, you say "if I act the way I really want to act, she might not flirt with me, and she might ignore me; Therefore, I must play up to her ego in order to keep getting attention from her...." *She has you changing your natural behavior in order to please and flatter HER ego!!! You just got egotistically punked.*

- You want a woman's attention and companionship so bad, that you spend hundreds of dollars on wining & dining her, even though she hasn't expressed any desire in dating you, or going to bed with you; Why? Because in your mind, you say "I have to earn some 'brownie points'; Otherwise, I'm afraid she won't 'like me' as much" *She has you treating her to free lunches, dinners, concerts,etc., when she has no real plans of being physical with you!!! You just got egotistically punked.*

- You meet a woman, and ask for her phone number; She says, "I don't give out my phone number, but you can give me yours..." What do you do? Enthusiastically write down your phone number. Why? Because in your mind, you say "if I don't give her my number, I'm afraid I'll never see or hear from that woman again. I'll do damn near anything to attract and maintain that woman's attention." *95-99% chance, you will never hear from that woman!! She just wanted to see how bad you want her attention!!! You just got egotistically punked.*

In my mind, *conquering your fears* is ten times more important than whether or not a woman has sex with you on the first date.

• *I like most of what you express in "Mode One: Let The Women Know What You're REALLY Thinking," but I feel uncomfortable approaching a woman, and immediately expressing my erotic desires in an explicit, graphic, kinky, and/or raunchy manner; I don't want to be perceived as crass, rude, disrespectful, or highly promiscuous. How do I avoid this??*

First of all, exhibiting Mode One Behavior is not specifically about going up to a woman and immediately talking about sex in an "XXX-rated" manner. **THIS IS PROBABLY THE BIGGEST MISCONCEPTION ABOUT MODE ONE.** In Chapter 6, I mention that I am a fan of John Leslie's character of "Jack" in the Classic adult film, "Talk Dirty To Me," because the character of Jack is so "Mode One." But realistically, you can be "Mode One" while using PG-rated language, PG-13 rated language, or R-rated language. You don't have to use X-rated, or XXX-rated language in order to be upfront and straightforward about a desire to have [casual] sex, or to let a woman know you're interested in dating her.

I have to set the record straight though: ALL HEALTHY, HETEROSEXUAL MEN WANT TO HAVE SEX WITH WOMEN. Don't be intimidated when a woman says "Is that all you think about ... sex???" Look her dead in her eyes, and say "YES." Women crack me up trying to prevent MEN FROM BEING MEN.

I've heard women say things like "I don't particularly care for a man who just thinks about sex...." That's crap. **Women love sex just as much as men.** Don't ever be fooled. All dating relationships are ultimately about **sexual attraction** and **erotic tension.** "What about romance?" *What about it?* When you have a "romantic" interest in a woman, all that means is that

148

you want her to have sex <u>EXCLUSIVELY</u> with YOU on a long-term basis. It's still based on **sexual chemistry.** "What about love? Emotional attachment?" **What is LOVE without SEXUAL CHEMISTRY??** **PLATONIC LOVE.** There are only three types of "love": Spiritual/family love, platonic love, and sexual love. *You don't date a woman, or marry a woman, because of spiritual and/or platonic love.* You marry them because *you have some degree of interest in having <u>sex</u> with them.*

Not all men have "promiscuous" intentions, or desires for "one-night stands" or casual sex. We live in a society where the HIV virus is rampant. **You have to use common sense, and be sexually responsible.** But that doesn't mean that they can't express their other desires, interests, and intentions in the most highly self-assured, and straightforward manner. And truthfully, it's not the "kinky," sexually provocative talk that turns women on anyway. When you exhibit Mode One, even if you are using sexually explicit language, that's not really what gets them aroused, assuming they get aroused; It's the BOLD, "BALLS OUT" BEHAVIOR that results from **egotistical indifference** that gets them aroused. I've had many women confess this to me. "Sex talk," without a confident demeanor to back it up, means nothing. **BOLD CONFIDENCE turns women on.** When you say anything, sexual or non-sexual, that women know requires BIG A** BALLS to say, that turns them on. Matter of fact, I've had at least a half-dozen women who have communicated to me that "Alan … you want to know what really turns me on in a man? What I really think makes a man 'sexy'?? **It's a man who DOESN'T REALLY CARE WHAT OTHER PEOPLE THINK OF HIM.** Those guys are usually very COCKY and very BOLD." Women get turned on by men who are highly confident, will speak their mind in a straightforward manner, and will make no apologies for behavior that is not met with an enthusiastic reaction. Why? Because this means that you're **EGOTISTICALLY INDIFFERENT.** You're not afraid of being criticized or disliked. You're not afraid of being "rejected" or ignored. You're not seeking 'approval' from everyone by being overly deferential and flattering.

Forget the emphasis on kinky sex talk. You can tell a woman "I'm sexually attracted to you" rather than say "I want to fu** you." When exhibiting Mode One, your emphasis should be on *conquering your fears, and behaving the way you REALLY want to behave,* instead of behaving in the manner that you think will be the most "pleasing," "flattering," and/or "accommodating" to a woman's ego. But remember though, whether your interests are centered around a long-term, romantic relationship, or a short-term, casual sex interaction, they're both based on **erotic tension** and **sexual chemistry**.

- *Is it possible to 'start out' using Mode Two Behavior, and then 'gradually' progress to using Mode One Behavior with a woman??*

For the most part, I would have to say NO. I'm not going to say that's "impossible," but that's extremely difficult. Primarily, because part of exhibiting Mode One Behavior means expressing your true desires, interests, and intentions to a woman IMMEDIATELY. When you're not UPFRONT, and you wait until the third or fourth conversation to confidently and straightforwardly express your true interests, then that's just a more confident variation of Mode Two Behavior. YOU'RE NOT AS FEARFUL THEN.

The problem I have with Mode Two Behavior is that it usually keeps the woman in "egotistical control" of her interactions with you. For the most part, she will be basically "calling the shots." Mode Two is a fear-based form of behavior. Mode Two is primarily predicated on a fear of being harshly criticized, or disliked. When you exhibit Mode Two Behavior, you want to first prove to a woman who you're a "good guy," a "gentleman," a "trustworthy" guy, a "classy" guy, and a "likable" guy, before you finally express what your true romantic and/or sexual desires are. You're afraid that if you're too straightforward too quickly, that it will "turn a woman off," and you'll have negative or critical things said about you behind your back.

SO WHAT. You know what type of person you are. Who cares about other people's perceptions and opinions about your behavior. **YOU CAN'T PLEASE EVERYBODY.**

- *Mode One seems like it would work only on unrefined, promiscuous, and/or naïve women; I can't see a classy, highly educated, professional woman with a decent set of morals and values reacting positively to the blunt, provocative straightforwardness of Mode One Behavior. Right or wrong??*

Any man who's exhibited Mode One Behavior towards a number of women, knows that this is **far from true**. Some of the most enthusiastic responses I've received from women after exhibiting Mode One Behavior were from intelligent, educated, "classy" women. Matter of fact, ironically, it's usually the "unrefined" women who give you the most NEGATIVE reactions. Hey ... classy, intelligent, educated women want to date, marry, and have orgasms too. Don't be silly.

Similar to this, I've had men say, "Alan ... I approached this classy, professional-type woman, and expressed my romantic and sexual desires to her in the most confident, and straightforward manner as possible . . . . . and then, she started 'going off' on me. Cursing me out, criticizing my moral upbringing, calling me 'shallow' and 'promiscuous,' and so on and so on. I then apologized, and felt very regretful." Shame, shame, shame. YOU'RE A VERBAL WIMP. Listen to this, and listen to me good:

NEVER, EVER BECOME APOLOGETIC and/or DEFENSIVE in response to a woman's SUBJECTIVE CRITICISMS and/or OPINIONATED INSULTS. All she's doing is TESTING YOU!!!! (Think about Wholesome Pretenders and Erotic Hypocrites)

That's right. When a woman starts going into 10, 20, or 30 minutes of harsh criticism about your cocky, provocatively straightforward behavior, all she's doing is TESTING THE STRENGTH OF YOUR EGO, and the SIZE OF YOUR BALLS. She's seeing if you're real, or "faking the funk" (i.e., "pretending" to be boldly confident, when deep down, you're really not).

I can count at least two dozen times that I've had a woman INITIALLY criticize me (sometimes, very harshly), only to *later on* end up getting together with me, and even dating me or having sex with me. **If a woman was 100% not interested** in you, she wouldn't **take the time to criticize you or insult you.** She would just immediately <u>end the conversation</u> and proceed to <u>ignore you</u>.

If a woman is able to cause you to apologize for your behavior as a direct result of her criticisms, what does that tell a female subconsciously?? **"I CAN MANIPULATE, INTIMIDATE, AND CONTROL THIS MAN WITH CRITICISM. HE IS AFRAID OF BEING CRITICIZED or DISLIKED BY ME."** Don't be a verbal wimp ... ALL YOUR LIFE.

• *What if I am attracted to a co-worker, or business colleague of mine, and I want to express my romantic and/or sexual interests to her in a confident, straightforward manner, but I don't want to risk being accused of "sexual harassment"???*

Generally speaking, I would say that you should **ALWAYS AVOID** expressing romantic and sexual desires to a co-worker or subordinate. The rules regarding sexual harassment these days are crazy and out of control. I wouldn't even dare risk expressing a desire to be physically romantic or sexual with a woman in the workplace. The consequences are just too great.

I actually have "mixed" feelings on the whole idea of sexual harassment. On one end, I don't believe ANY WOMAN should ever be truly **HARASSED**. By "harassed," I mean having a guy **PERSISTENTLY** make **unwanted** romantic and/or sexual advances to a woman who works with him, or for him.

But many accusations of "sexual harassment" are NOT really representative of "harassment." I've heard of women wanting to accuse a male co-worker or supervisor of sexual harassment simply for asking them out on a date, or telling them that their dress was sexy. **That's crap**. A **one-time** comment, question, or advance is <u>NOT</u> harassment. To harass a woman means to **repeatedly** and **persistently** make advances towards a woman after a woman has *ALREADY let you know that she's not interested*. Sorry though. This book is not about harassment.

You have to use **common sense**.

GLOSSARY

<u>Note</u>: While these terms may have certain meanings apparent to the lay public, this glossary is added for clarification of the meanings as particularly applied in this book.

Alpha Male Syndrome (AMS): When a man takes on the animal-like attitude that the most physically dominant males should have the highest degree of popularity with the most desirable women, and that less dominant males should 'submit' to their authority and influence. *(Chapter Seven)*

Dark Side: That aspect of a person's character or personality that is inherently evil, immoral, or perverted. Usually is revealed when a man is in a Mode Four state of mind. *(Chapter Five)*

"Dissed": A slang term that is a variation of "disrespected"; When a man or woman fails to acknowledge your presence, and/or fails to reciprocate your desires and interests, in a blatantly disrespectful manner. *(Chapter Five)*

"Dr. Jekyll & Mr. Hyde" Behavior: Based on the characters created by *Robert Louis Stevenson* (1886), this is the behavior that is attributed to a man who frequently vacillates between Mode Two Behavior and Mode Four Behavior. *(Chapter Five)*

Effective Behavior: Any form of behavior you exhibit that is highly conducive to the achievement of your desired goals and objectives. For example, when you express your desires, interests, and intentions in an honest, straightforward, and upfront manner.

Egotistical Indifference: The primary basis for exhibiting Mode One Behavior. When you're "egotistically indifferent," this means that you never become too excited in response to flattery, nor do you feel too offended or dejected by subjective criticisms or opinionated insults. When a man allows his ego to become 'too attached' to receiving a specific type of reaction or response from women, this is what ultimately causes his fears of criticism and rejection.

Erotic Hypocrites (EHs):   Manipulative women who possess a specific desire to date and marry men who have a high degree of wealth, education, and social status;   They will generally hide their true sexual interests and sexual history from their potential mates, as well as harshly criticize men and other women for engaging in free-spirited sexual practices, even though they enjoy unconventional forms of sexual pleasure themselves.   *(Chapter Six)*

Erotic Tension: Basically, the cause of sexual chemistry.   Erotic tension usually develops when one's ego is challenged and/or frustrated by the behavior of a member of the opposite sex.   Bold, provocative behavior usually creates erotic tension.

"Gentleman":   A man who is perceived as honorable, courteous, considerate, and exceptionally well-mannered and polite.   This is usually the image that all men who exhibit Mode Two Behavior strive for.   *(Chapter Three)*

Ineffective Behavior: Any behavior that you exhibit that is counterproductive to the achievement of your desired goals and objectives;   For example, when you express your desires, interests, and intentions in a cautious, indirect, and/or deceitful manner.

Manipulative Behavior: Behavior that is not totally honest, but at the same time, not totally dishonest;   Usually involves either the use of tangible and intangible "incentives" and "rewards," or the use of deceptive, misleading behavior, in an attempt to achieve a self-serving objective. *(Chapter Two)*

Misogyny / Misogynistic Behavior: When a man is physically and sexually attracted to women, but has a deep felt hatred and lack of respect for females as human beings.   Men who exhibit Mode Four Behavior are typically misogynists. *(Chapter Five)*

"Nice" Behavior: Behavior that, on the positive side, is generally polite, friendly, enthusiastic, and entertaining, but on the negative side, is usually too lenient, too cautious, and/or too accommodating. Usually exhibited by a Mode Two "Gentleman." (*Chapter Three*)

Platonic Interest: When a person is interested in communicating with you, and sharing your company, on a regular or semi-regular basis, but in a totally non-romantic, non-sexual manner. (*Chapter Three*)

Player Hater: A person who dislikes others for no other reason than the fact they are jealous and envious of their social status, level of career and financial success, and/or their degree of popularity with others. (*Chapter Seven*)

Real Behavior: Behavior that is representative of your true desires, interests, intentions, and character; Behavior that is devoid of any phony or pretentious airs. (*Chapter Eight*)

Romantic Interest: When a person is interested in communicating with you, and sharing your company, within the context of a committed, monogamous sexual relationship (*Chapter Two*)

Sexual Interest: When a person is interested in sharing your company for the primary, if not specific purpose, of exchanging pleasurable orgasms. (*Chapter Two*)

Small Talk: Any conversation that you engage in with another that is usually trivial and meaningless, but to some degree, entertaining; The content of the conversation has nothing to do with your needs, desires, long-term intentions, or true interests. (*Chapter One*)

Strong Behavior: Any form of behavior you exhibit that makes it virtually impossible for others to manipulate you, disrespect you, and/or cause you to change or compromise your personal principles and values without a valid purpose.

Targets: A man who frequently exhibits Mode Three Behavior that usually has a high degree of wealth and social status; These men will typically engage in a lot of pretentious, uninteresting small talk with women which usually revolves around what they own, what they've accomplished, and what they have to offer financially and materialistically. *(Chapter Four)*

Timids: A man who frequently exhibits Mode Three Behavior that usually has very little, if any, courage or self-confidence; These men will typically avoid approaching and interacting with women altogether. *(Chapter Four)*

Unapologetically Straightforward: When a man is exhibiting Mode One Behavior (or Mode Four Behavior), and he expresses his desires, interests, and intentions in an extremely unambiguous and forthright manner, without giving any hint of shame or regret for their manner of expression. *(Chapter Eight)*

Verbal Wimp: A person who allows their fear of being criticized, disliked, rejected, or ignored to prevent them from expressing their true desires, interests, and intentions to others in an honest, confident, upfront, and straightforward manner. *(Chapter Four)*

Weak Behavior: Any form of behavior you exhibit that makes it fairly easy for others to manipulate you, disrespect you, and/or provoke you to change or compromise your personal principles and values without valid cause.

Wholesome Pretenders (WPs): Manipulative women who give off the public impression that they are the living personification of wholesomeness, chaste, sexual conservatism, and monogamous virtues, when in reality, these same women have frequently experienced "one-night stands" and "casual flings." *(Chapter Six)*

Other Books I Would Recommend

As I mentioned in my acknowledgements, there are a number of other authors whose books, philosophies, knowledge, and wisdom either directly, or indirectly, influenced many of my own principles and philosophies represented in this book. Inevitably, I'm going to leave someone out, but here is my list of books you might want to take a look at, that I consider to be high-quality:

James Allen: *"As A Man Thinketh"*

Michael Baisden: *"Never Satisfied: How & Why Men Cheat"*

Dr. Brad Blanton: *"Radical Honesty: How To Transform Your Life By Telling The Truth"*

Dr. Harriet B. Braiker: *"Who's Pulling Your Strings? How To Break The Cycle of Manipulation and Regain Control of Your Life"* and *"The Disease To Please"*

Kelly Bryson: *"Don't Be Nice, Be Real: Balancing Passion For Self with Compassion for Others"*

Dr. Susan Campbell: *"Getting Real: Ten Truth Skills You Need to Live An Authentic Life"*

Stephen R. Covey: *"The 7 Habits Of Highly Effective People"* and *"The 8th Habit: From Effectiveness to Greatness"*

Jon Favreau: *"Swingers: The Swingers' Rules and a Screenplay"*

Dr. Susan Forward (with Donna Frazier): *"Emotional Blackmail: When the People In Your Life Use Fear, Obligation, and Guilt to Manipulate You"*

Dr. Susan Jeffers: *"Feel The Fear and Do It Anyway"*

Alfie Kohn: *"Punished By Rewards: The Trouble With Gold Stars, Incentive Plans, A's, Praise, and Other Bribes"*

Rom Wills: *"Nice Guys & Players: Becoming The Man Women Want"*

Lightning Source UK Ltd.
Milton Keynes UK
19 October 2010

161538UK00001B/164/A